VIENNA

KOMPASS Guide

© **KOMPASS-Karten GmbH • 6063 Rum/Innsbruck, Austria**

Third edition, 2004
Publisher's No. 521
ISBN 3-85491-348-6

CONTENTS

WELCOME TO VIENNA!

No matter what has led or will lead you to Vienna – whether it is the desire to explore the capital of Austria for yourself (having already heard such a lot about it), or whether it is a visit to a performance in the State Opera House or to one of the well-known theatres, or perhaps you simply want to go shopping – whatever it is, this booklet will help you to get where you want to go. On the other hand you may find some suggestions that will lead you to places you have never heard of before; you may discover something new, experience the vibrant life of this city, today one of the most active in Europe.

If your time is short, you should take a look at the chapter "Exploring Vienna". There is surely time for at least one of the "10 Sights Not to be Missed". Let us stay with this chapter for a moment: with a few exceptions, mainly sights in the Inner City, in the 1st District, are described here. If you have only one day for your visit to Vienna, you can explore this central district and oldest part of town by following the walking tours. Here we are confronted with the magnificent era of the Habsburg empire as well as the development of spleandour in architecture, from Gothic to Baroque to historicism and Jugendstil (Art Nouveau).

Other visitors to Vienna feel drawn to one of the famous museums. In the chapter "Museums" you can get an impression of the abundance of culture and art treasures that have accumulated (throughout the centuries) and that are still being collected in the former royal capital. Here you can get an idea of the wealth and variety of Austrian and occidental culture.

If you are travelling with children, there is absolutely no need to do without all the pleasures of culture and feel you have to search for children's playgrounds in Vienna. You can find tips in the section "Children's Favourites". The suggestions here are just as appealing to adults, they are of interest to both the old and the young (with the exception of the children's open-air swimming pools, where only children are allowed in!). What is still missing for a successful stay in Austria's capital? Useful tips as to where you can find some refreshment after all the walking tours and the sightseeing? Or where you can do some physical exercise after all the strain on your intellect? There are quite a number of sports facilities in Vienna. In the section on information you can also find ideas on where you can spend the evenings and nights.

Important telephone numbers and addresses are included.

KOMPASS

◀ *Bird's-eye view of the city's heartthrob: the Cathedral of St. Stephen*

A SURVEY OF AUSTRIA'S CAPITAL CITY

GEOGRAPHY – GEOLOGY – CLIMATE

The city spreads across the western rim of the Vienna Basin which stretches from the eastern foothills of the Alps to the vast Hungarian lowland plain. The position on the Danube, the most important west-east connection in Europe in living memory, and on the "amber trail", the north-south axis between the Baltic Sea and the Adriatic, running through the Vienna Basin, have very much favoured the origin and the further development of Vienna – from the Roman camp Vindobona to the ducal and imperial residence of the Babenbergs and Habsburgs. After the First Word War a change came about. From the metropolis of a world power Vienna was now the capital of Austria, a country much reduced in size. Vienna remained the political, economic, spiritual and cultural centre of the Alpine republic.

The federal capital is the seat of the federal president and the federal government, of the "Nationalrat" (the Lower Chamber in Austria's parliament) and the "Bundesrat" (the Upper Chamber). It is also the seat of the Supreme Court and of several United Nations organisations. In 1922 the city of Vienna was proclaimed a separate Austrian federal province; since then the mayor of Vienna is also the provincial governor and the district council acts as the provincial government and holds its meetings in the conference room of the town hall. On the globe you can find Vienna at a latitude of 48° 14' north and at a longitude of 16° 21' east. It lies at 171 m above mean sea level (St. Stephen's Cathedral), the highest point is on Hermannskogel, 542 m, the lowest in the Lobau, 151 m. The area of about 415 km^2 is surrounded by the federal province of Lower Austria. The city, which has grown continuously, is today divided into 23 districts:

1. Innere Stadt
2. Leopoldstadt
3. Landstrasse
4. Wieden
5. Margareten
6. Mariahilf
7. Neubau
8. Josefstadt
9. Alsergrund
10. Favoriten
11. Simmering
12. Meidling
13. Hietzing
14. Penzing
15. Rudolfsheim-Fünfhaus
16. Ottakring
17. Hernals
18. Währing
19. Döbling
20. Brigittenau
21. Floridsdorf
22. Donaustadt
23. Liesing

The 1st District is the "Altstadt" of Vienna, the old city centre that lay

View from Leopoldsberg

within the city walls and where most of the historically important buildings can be found. The 3rd to 9th Districts are the "inner-city districts" that have developed from the former suburbs. The "outlying" districts are numbered 10 to 19 and used to be suburbs outside the "Gürtel" (the outer ring road); the 2nd District and Districts 20 to 22 are beyond the Danube Canal or the Danube itself, and the 23rd District is on the southern outskirts of the city.

Each district has its own individual characteristic: the 3rd District, for example, is the diplomats' quarter, the 1st and the 4th are the most elegant areas in town, the rising bourgeoisie has left its stamp on the 5th, 6th and 7th District and the 8th has always been favoured as the residential area for officials. Doctors' surgeries, hospitals and sanatoriums are to be found in the 9th District, and the 18th District, Währing, is a popular residential area.

With a population of 1,562,500 million Vienna is not one of today's largest cities although it was still one of the six largest in the world at the onset of the 20th century, when it had 2 million inhabitants. In the days "When Bohemia was still part of Austria" people of various ethnic origins flocked to the capital to work and to live. After the First World War the population decreased steadily. Nowadays, however, the number of inhabitants is definitely on the increase (influx from other Austrian states, immigrants since the fall of the Iron Curtain), and by the year 2010 a population of 1.7 million is expected again. The city of Vienna has to provide 120,000 apartments as well as create new businesses in the next two decades. Another important task for the city's administration is to renovate the Inner City with its run-down flats in old buildings. A whole district, Spittelberg in the 7th District, has been beautifully redeveloped.

The improvement of the quality of life within the city is an objective of great importance: pedestrian precincts, extension of the underground (U-Bahn) and suburban fast trains (S-Bahn) and Park + Ride-System are to reduce motor traffic. Vienna can also be described as a "green" city: 50% of the municipal area is green zone, 32% is developed area, 14 % is traffic surface and 4 % is covered by water and waterways.

One quarter of all working people are employed in the federal capital, Austria's largest **economic centre** and almost all branches of production are represented here (90% are medium-sized and small businesses). The traditional industrial branches are concerned with manufacturing and processing raw materials. The food, tobacco and alcohol industries have the largest turnover; precision engineering, electro mechanics and the metal-processing industry are of the greatest importance. The production of china and leather goods as well as the variety of goods produced in the craft industry are world-famous. Tourism prospers in the Austrian capital mainly because ot its cultural and historical importance, many visitors come from other parts of Austria and from abroad.

It is generally recognized that Vienna is one of the most important **cultural centres** in the world. Architecture, painting, poetry and, above all, music have always flourished here. In no other city have so many important composers lived and worked, from no other city has so much music been produced. It was here that classical music was perfected by such men as Joseph Haydn, Wolfgang Amadeus Mozart and Ludwig van Beethoven (Viennese classic). The "song prince" Franz Schubert was himself a child of this city. In the 19th century the Viennese waltz reached its peak with Josef Lanner and the Strauss family. Composers such as Johannes Brahms, Anton Bruckner, Gustav Mahler, Arnold Schönberg and Alban Berg continued in the classical tradition right into the 20th century. Vienna has first-class orchestras, the world-famous Philharmonic and Symphonic Orchestras and a number of other orchestras and chamber music ensembles and at least 20 choirs – with the traditional Vienna Boys' Choir at the top of the list. Internationally renowned singers and conducters make guest appearances at the Viennese State Opera House.

The **university** (Alma Mater Rudolphina), founded as early as 1365, is of international significance, especially in the fields of medicine, psychology, physics and engineering.

Geology

The main part of the municipal area is situated on the western slopes of the Vienna Basin which forms a terrace-like transition to the hills of the Vienna Woods. The Vienna Basin is a zone which caved in to a depth of about 5,000 m during the Tertiary period. It was flooded by the sea that covered large sections of what is now Austria and was filled with sediments. The so-called "Thermal Line" runs along the fault zones where mineral hot springs (Baden,

The Romans were Vienna's first vintners

Bad Vöslau) occur. Fault systems underground – the "Leopoldsdorf Fault" – are the reason why the largest oil and natural gas fields in Central Europe are located within Vienna's city limits (Aderklaa, Süssenbrunn, Oberlaa, Kagran). In the southwest the city spreads over on to the Vienna Woods which count as part of the eastern foothills of the Eastern Alps. The Vienna Woods belong to the Flysch Zone which borders the Calcareous Alps to the north. The adjacent Northern Calcareous Alps form the Rax and Schneeberg massifs. This is where the Austrian capital gets most of its drinking water from (1st Viennese aqueduct). The crystalline of the Semmering and the Bucklige Welt borders the Vienna Basin to the south and southeast and continues on to the Rosalien and Leitha mountains.

The Ice Ages had an indirect effect on the Vienna area. After the Danube breached the Viennese Gate ("Wiener Pforte"), between Kahlenberg and Bisamberg, it eroded the tertiary gravel and sand. The ice-age debris was transported along by the meltwater. Through subsequent erosion the sediments were carved out in the course of the different glaciation periods forming a series of glacial terraces. The succession of terraces corresponds to the different glaciation periods – the lowest, and thus the most recent, is the Prater Terrace. The Danube's meanders cut through these layers after the last Ice Age. The tributaries and brooks (e. g. Wien, Liesing, Alserbach, Ottakringer Bach) formed the landscape, till finally, from the Early Stone Age on, human beings also left their mark on the countryside. The City Terrace was chosen as a place for settlement (175 m, today approx. 20 m above the level of the Danube) as it was high enough above the floodplain of the Danube. Today's Inner City developed around the old core settlement. The growing city with its incorporated suburbs spread out across the terraces as far as the Vienna Woods. The Alpine setting and the tertiary debris of the Vienna Basin supplied various kinds of building material that can be seen all over the city. For example, the Romans used the Flysch sandstone for building and sands from the older tertiary layers were excavated in Heiligenstadt and on the Türkenschanze. Clay from the clay pits of the former Pannonian Sea was used to make bricks in the Wienerberg brick factories in the southern part of the city. Leitha limestone (older layers from tertiary sediments), from eastern Lower Austria and Burgenland, was used to build several of the city's monumental edifices such as the Votive Church, the University, the State Opera House and a great part of St. Stephen's Cathedral (the Imperial Quarry/Kaisersteinbruch), the Roman Quarry/Römersteinbruch in St. Margarethen among others.

Fine Aeolian sand that came from the debris that was deposited beyond the moraines in outwash plains during the Ice Age is known as Loess. This Loess was blown by the wind and settled in the subsoil over a large area, thus forming the fertile ground for the traditional viniculture.

Climate

Due to Vienna's position at the eastern edge of the arch of the Alps and to the opening towards the east to the Pannonian area, the yearly weather depends on the one hand on oceanic, on the other on continental influences. Whether the oceanic weather pattern or the eastern European high pressure zone dominates depends on the distribution of pressure. The climate in Vienna, therefore, is predominatly of a moderate, continental type: generally cold winters and hot summers and not a great deal of precipitation. Frost can be expected from December till March. In July and August, the temperature can climb to over 30°C, though heat waves and cold spells never last very long. Precipitation is distributed evenly over the whole year, autumn is the season of the least precipitation: warm, fair weather in September as well as damp foggy days promote the quality of the wine. An almost proverbial "Vienna breeze" keeps the otherwise unavoidable traditional big-city haze and winter smog away.

Giant Ferris Wheel in Prater: one of Vienna's landmarks ▶

5000 BC
Traces of human culture discovered on the Bisamberg, north-east of Vienna.

3500 – 1800 BC (Neolithic Age)
Permanent settlements in the Vienna area in the region of today's Schönbrunn, Leopoldau and Aspern. Indo-Germanic peoples from North Germany then settle on the hills to the west and on the terrace that slopes down steeply to the River Danube (the Hoher Markt area in the 1st District).

Around 400 BC (New Iron Age, La-Tène-Age)
Celts from the east of France and from the central Rhine region move to the Vienna area, to the city terrace above the Danube (today the region Hoher Markt) **Celtic settlement "Vindobona"** – named either after the Vinide tribe or after the Celtic word "Vedunia" (= forest stream), the Wien River.

15 BC
Under Emperor Augustus the **Romans** occupy the Eastern Alpine Region as far as the Danube.

14 – 37 AD
Under Emperor Tiberius the oldest and strongest Roman military camp in Austria develops east of Vienna: Carnuntum, the capital of Pannonia.

41 – 54 AD
Under Emperor Claudius the Limes (border rampart) is built alongside the Danube. **Roman camp Vindobona** for military auxiliary troops (in today's 3rd District).

115 AD
Under Emperor Trajan the X. Legion is stationed in the fortified camp Vindobona (today the area Hoher Markt). In place of the Celtic town Vedunia, Roman civilian town with approx. 20.000 inhabitants (area south-east of today's Belvedere)

167 – 180
In the wars against the Germanic Marcomanni **Emperor Marc Aurel** successfully defended the Vienna Basin. Marc Aurel dies around 180 in Vindobona.

Roman excavations at Michaelerplatz

213
Vindobona acquires Roman city status.

395
After the destruction of Carnuntum by the Quadi **Vindobona becomes the military and economic centre of the Danube area,** the Roman Danube fleet is based here.

400 – 433
Vindobona is destroyed by Visigoths, but settled again. The **Huns** capture Pannonia – the Romans withdraw for good.

500 – 700
Bavarians, various Germanic tribes from Böhmen, migrate to the foothills of the Alps and gradually advance to the Viennese Woods.

788
Charlemagne dismisses the Bavarian Duke Tassilo III. After the victory over the Avars, he founds the Pannonine (Carolingian) March, the earl's residence is at Tulln.

881
The first official reference to Vienna – "ad weniam" – appears in the annals of Salzburg.

907
The East March (Ostmark) declines after the defeat of the Bavarians against the Magyar (= Hungary) near Pressburg – Vienna under Hungarian rule till 991. The Hungarian name for Vienna "Becs" (this means town on the steep rim) is still used today.

955
Emperor Otto I defeats the Magyars in the decisive battle at the Lechfeld.

976
Babenberg Liutpold the first margrave from the East March of the "eastern land" (Ostland) (as from 996 Ostrarichi).

991
Further extension of the East March to the Vienna Basin, around 1039 as far as March and Leitha. Residence again Tulln.

996
Ostarrichi (eastern kingdom), Österreich (Austria), officially mentioned in a document.

1030
After lost battle Vienna conquered temporarily by Hungary. Bavarian border fortress "Wiennis" officially mentioned.

1095 – 1136
Under **Margrave Leopold III the Saint** (canonized in 1485) Vienna becomes a city with a provincial sovereign (the House of Babenberg) and an important port. In 1106 the residence is transferred from Tulln to the Leopoldsberg north of Vienna. The Abbey of Klosterneuburg is founded at the foot of the residence around 1107.

1147
Inauguration by Bishop Reginbert von Passau of the **Parish Church St. Stephan,** founded outside the city walls.

1155 – 1158
Duke Henry II Jasomirgott transfers the Babenberg's residence to Vienna. He founds his Palace "Am Hof" and the Scots Abbey (Schottenstift) in 1158.

1198 – 1230
Under Leopold VI, the Glorious, the city flourishes due to trade with the Orient via Venice, as a result of viniculture and as a trade centre for cloth, salt and precious metals from Flanders – thus conversion of the city to a **trading city** (with squares such as Neuer Markt, Judenplatz) and extension of the municipal area to the south. As far as

the church is concerned, Vienna still belongs to the diocese Passau. The Duke's Court is transferred to the area of today's Stallburg. Promotion of the courtly art of poetry (Minnesänger Walther von der Vogelweide, Ulrich von Liechtenstein, Neidhart von Reuenthal).

1221
Vienna is granted a **city charter as well as a trade monopoly.**

1237 – 1239
During the conflict between Duke Friedrich II and the German emperor Vienna becomes an "Imperial Free City" (Privileges!), later to be recaptured by the Babenbergs.

1246
Duke Friedrich II is killed in the battle of the Leitha against the Hungarians – thus dies the last of the House of Babenberg. Vienna is again an imperial free city for a short time.

1246 – 1276
After a dispute as to who should rule, the Bohemian Prince **Ottokar II Premysl** takes on the Austrian provinces in 1250. He has the city rebuilt in 1262 after a fire disaster. Beginning of the construction of the Hofburg and the new city walls, fourth extension of the city. Ottokar II refuses to surrender his acquisitions to King Rudolf von Habsburg as feudal lord. Rudolf besieges Vienna, which is on Ottokar's side, for weeks on end. Temporary peace agreement.

1278
Ottokar is slain in the Battle of Marchfeld. The reign of **Rudolf I** over Austria marks the beginning of almost 640 years of Habsburg rule (till 1918). With Rudolf Vienna is once again an imperial free city.

1282
Rudolf enfeoffs his sons with Austria and Styria, thus founding the dynastic power of the Habsburgs. Vienna's first mayor is Konrad Poll.

1350
First **outbreak of the Plague** annihilates 1/3 of the population.

1358 – 1365
The reign of **Rudolf IV the Founder** finds Vienna competing with Karl IV's Prague – cultural and economic development of Vienna.
Guilds no longer compulsory. In order to obtain money for building projects, taxes (on land, property and drinks) are introduced.

1365
The **University** of Vienna is founded by Duke Rudolf IV – after Prague the second oldest in the German-speaking world.

1421
Persecution of the Jews.
Destruction of the Ghetto (Quarter around the Judenplatz).

1438
Albrecht II (the Austrian Duke Albrecht V) becomes King of the Germans and with him Vienna becomes the capital of the Holy Roman Empire of the German Nation.

1469
Founding of the diocese of Vienna.

1485 – 1490
The Hungarian King **Matthew Corvinus** occupies Vienna. After his death **Maximilian I** (the son of Emperor Friedrich III) moves to Vienna (1490).

1493 – 1519
After the death of his father Maximilian becomes the Holy Roman Emperor and Archduke of Austria; humanism at its peak, art, science

and music are promoted at the imperial court. The "Hofmusikkapelle" (Court Orchestra), forerunner of the Vienna Boys' Choir, is established.

1525
A **devastating fire** destroys about 40% of the houses in the city.

1529
The **Turks** under Sultan Suleiman II besiege Vienna for the first time – the Viennese under the command of Count Niklas of Salm. The cold October weather forces the Turks to withdraw after 3 weeks. Result of this siege: rapid improvement of Vienna's hitherto weak fortifications including a wide embankment.

1541
1/3 of the population again become victims of the **Plague.**

1551
Jesuits summoned to Vienna – strong impact on the schools and university and in the **Counter-Reformation** that begins in **1576,** and starts out from here. Main representatives Cardinal Melchior Khlesl (as from 1598 Archbishop of Vienna, 1611 – 1681 the emperor's chancellor).
Rudolf II moves his court to Prague.

1618 – 1648
In the Thirty Years' War Bohemian Protestants in 1619 and Swedish troops in 1645 fail to break through Vienna's fortifications.

1666
Leopold I's wedding festivities with the Spanish Infantin Margareta Theresia last one whole year.

1679
The Plague once again claims 30.000 lives. The legend of the "lieber Augustin" (dear Augustin) finds its origin.

1683
2nd Turkish siege under grand vizier Kara Mustafa (14. July till 12. September). The Viennese under Count Starhemberg are freed by an army of 80,000 men under the Polish King Sobieski and Duke Charles of Loraine – the decisive battle on 12th September takes place in the region of today's Türkenschanzpark (19th District).
Some of the bags of coffee the Turks left behind lead to the opening of the first Viennese coffee house.

1683 – 1736
The victorious general **Prince Eu-**

Hackney cab in front of the Hofburg

gene of Savoy, the "valiant knight" restores the glory of a "Vienna gloriosa" to the capital of the empire.

1685 – 1780
The golden age of Baroque architecture, sculpture and painting in Vienna. Many buildings are constructed (castles, churches, palaces) under Leopold I, Joseph I, Charles VI and Maria Theresia. The famous architects of this era are Johann Bernhard Fischer von Erlach, his son Joseph Emanuel Fischer von Erlach and Lukas von Hildebrandt. The best-known sculptors are Georg Raphael Donner, Balthasar Ferdinand Moll and Franz Xaver Messerschmidt; artists worth mentioning are Johann Michael Rottmayr, Daniel Gran and Franz Anton Maulbertsch. Joseph Haydn and Wolfgang Amadeus Mozart are the musicians and composers of this golden age.

1722
Vienna becomes the seat of the archbishops.

1740 – 1780
Under **Maria Theresia** administration of the state is centralized in Vienna (world city). Progress in the field of education: the first elementary school as well as a spinning and weaving school are opened. In 1752 the Schönbrunn zoological garden is opened, the oldest menagerie in the world.

1754
First census in Vienna: approximately 175,000 civilians within the city walls.

1766
The "Prater" is opened to the public by Joseph II (co-regent since 1765).

1780 – 1790
Joseph II, the oldest son of Maria Theresia and Emperor Franz I von Lorraine, continues the line of the ruling House of Habsburg-Lorraine, though not his mother's pompous holding of court. His reign is marked by numerous reforms that partly exist to this day.

1782
Pope Pius VI in Vienna.

1805
Occupation of Vienna by the French.

1806
Franz II is forced by Napoleon to renounce the Holy Roman Imperial Crown. As from 1804 he is known as **Franz I,** Emperor of Austria.

1809
2nd occupation of Vienna by French troops – **Napoleon** in Schönbrunn Palace.

1812
Vienna counts 33 suburbs and about 240,000 inhabitants. War and occupying forces lead to national bankruptcy.

1814 – 1815
Congress of Vienna under the chairmanship of the state chancellor Prince Clemens Metternich – order is to be restored in Europe after Napoleon's abdication and exile.

1815 – 1848
The era of the "Vormärz" (historical period from 1815 to the March revolution of 1848) with its police informer system under Chancellor Metternich suppressed any liberal movement. Thus the **Biedermeier** style spread, above all in people's homes. Biedermeier art is to be found in furniture, china etc. Music-making in the home becomes widespread. Vienna's inhabitants enjoy going to the theatre (folk plays by Ferdinand Raimund and Johann Nestroy) and waltz music

by Josef Lanner and the Strauss dynasty is very popular.

1848

March Revolution – Metternich is forced to resign. In December Ferdinand I abdicates, his nephew **Franz Joseph I** is his successor.

1850 – 1873

"Gründerzeit" – numerous companies are founded, in the suburbs tenements lacking in any style ("Zinskasernen" – rented barracks) are built. The suburbs are incorporated into the city as far as the city walls, the city is extended by 8 districts (2nd-9th Districts).

When the bastions are razed to the ground (1857-1864) room is made to build the "Ringstrasse".

1873

World exhibition on today's "Messegelände" (exhibition grounds). Crash on the stock market.

1890

City walls pulled down. The suburbs (today 11th to 14th Districts) are incorporated into the city and a broad street, the "Gürtel" (belt) emerges.

1897 – 1910

Under Mayor Dr. Karl Lueger of the "christliche-soziale Partei" (Christian-Social Party) the expansion of Vienna to a modern city of the 20th century begins.

1916

Franz Joseph I dies in Schönbrunn Palace, his grand-nephew becomes his successor as Charles I.

1918

After the dissolution of the Dual Monarchy at the end of the First World War, the Republic is proclaimed, Vienna is the federal capital.

1922

Vienna becomes an Austrian federal state, the district council is also the Viennese "Landtag" (state parliament).

1923 – 1933

In the "Red Vienna" (majority in the Social Democratic Party) residential buildings and social reforms are pushed through – 60,000 apartments for the working class are built, among others the Karl-Marx-Hof.

1934

On 25th July Chancellor Engelbert Dollfuss is murdered in a coup attempt by the Nazis in the Federal Chancellory.

1938

German troops reach the capital. **Vienna is now "Reichsgau"** with 26 districts. 97 Lower Austrian communities are incorporated.

1939 – 1945

During the **Second World War** there is heavy damage caused by air raids and military clashes: about 11,000 Viennese lose their lives, 35,000 are left homeless, 21,000 houses are destroyed; shortly before the end of the war the State Opera is bombed and St. Stephan's Cathedral goes up in flames.

1945

The Soviet Red Army occupies Vienna. The city is divided into **4 occupation zones** (USSR, USA, Great Britain, France).

The 2nd Republic is proclaimed in Vienna and reconstruction begins under Mayor Theodor Körner.

1954

80 communities are returned to Lower Austria, only the 22nd and the 23rd Districts stay with Vienna.

1955

On 15th May the signing of the **Austrian International Treaty** with the occupying powers takes place in the Belvedere Palace: the occupying forces leave the country, Austria regains full sovereignty, a constitutional law for eternal neutrality is passed in Parliament.

1956
Vienna headquarters of the International Nuclear Energy Agency.

1961
John F. Kennedy and Nikita Chruschtschow meet in Vienna on 3rd/4th June.

1967
Vienna is headquarters of the United Nations Industrial Development Organisation (UNIDO).

1969
Construction of the underground railway commences.

1979
The UNO City is opened. US President Carter meets the President of the Soviet Union, Breschnew, in Vienna.

1983
Pope John Paul II in Vienna for the Assembly of Austrian Catholics.

1987
Opening of the conference centre "Austria Center Vienna" in the Danube Park. The Danube Island becomes Vienna's new leisure and recreation area.

1989
The people of Austria show their deep sympathy at the funeral of Zita of Habsburg, Austria's last empress, who died at the age of 96; burial in the Imperial Crypt in the Capuchin Monastery Church.

1992
Fire in the "Hofburg" (Imperial Palace), the Redouten Halls (Redoutensäle, ballrooms) are destroyed.

1997
Reopening of the renovated Redouten Halls.

2001
The MuseumsQuartier (MQ) Vienna is opened.

UNO-City

Fanciful municipal housing by Friedensreich Hundertwasser ▶

EXPLORING VIENNA

SIGHTS TO SEE FROM A – Z

The letter-number code refers to the coordinates on the city map (inside the front flap of this booklet).

(Akademie der bildenden Künste) Academy of Fine Arts

see Museums

(Akademie der Wissenschaften/ Alte Universität) Academy of Sciences – Old University   D 2/3

Jean Nicolas Jadot de Villelssey used the style of French rococo palaces for this building, constructed from 1753-1755, commissioned by Emperor Franz I. The ceiling paintings in the great hall, "Allegories of the Four Faculties" by Gregorio Guglielmi (1755) are reminiscent of the time this was a university building (till 1848). The ceiling painting in the former theology hall "Baptism of Christ" is by Franz Anton Maulbertsch. In 1857 the Academy of Sciences was founded here.

1st District, Dr.-Ignaz-Seipel-Platz 2

Memorial for the Victims of War and Fascism by Alfred Hrdlicka

Albertina *see Museums*

Albertinaplatz   C 3

This square borders an the Albrechts ramp – the remains of the Augustinian Bastion (city fortifications), taken down in 1858 – which crowns the **statue of Archduke Albrecht on horseback,** victor of the Battle of Custozza in 1866. The figures on the **Danubius Fountain** (1869) beneath allegorize the River Danube and its tributaries.
The **Memorial for the Victims of War and Fascism** by Alfred Hrdlicka (1988) reminds us of more recent history.

1st District

(Altes Rathaus) Old City Hall   C 2

This building served as the City Hall from the 13th century till 1883. Duke Frederick the Fair seized the property from the wealthy family Haymo and gave it to the City of Vienna. After extensions to the building, the facade was redesigned in a Baroque style around 1700, Johann Martin Fischer designed the portals at a later date. The council halls (Ratssäle) are ornamented with beautiful stuccoed ceilings. They are, however, only open to the public for special events. The Andromeda Fountain by Raphael Donner (1740/41) is in the courtyard. The Archives of the Austrian

10 Sights not to be missed!

★ **St. Stephen's Cathedral (Stephansdom)** a masterpiece of the Romanesque and Gothic styles and for centuries Vienna's most famous landmark; from the 137 m-high south spire ("Steffl") you can get a good view over the roofs and towers of the city.

★ The **Prater**, an extensive recreation area near the city centre. It is fun to take a ride on the **Giant Ferris Wheel (Riesenrad)** and to spend time in the amusement park, especially at night.

★ **(Kunsthistorisches Museum) Museum of Fine Art** and its extensive **Picture Gallery** are world-famous.

★ The splendid setting of the Baroque **Belvedere Palaces;** the museums in the palatial rooms give an excellent survey of Austrian painting and sculpture from the Middle Ages to the present.

★ The Secular and Ecclesiastical **Treasuries (Schatzkammer)** in the

Hofburg with its impressive collection of sovereign insignia.

★ The magnificent **Karlskirche (Church of St. Charles Borromeo)** one of the most splendid examples of Baroque architecture in Europe.

★ A day in **Schönbrunn:** the rooms in the Baroque imperial palace that are open to the public and the expansive park grounds with the Gloriette, a victory monument, the oldest zoo in the world (founded 1752), and the Palm House.

★ A visit to a **Viennese coffeehouse** – there are enough to chose from!

★ The Vienna **Naschmarkt** (fruit & vegetable market) and – only on Saturdays – the adjacent flea market.

★ The wonderful view from the **Kahlenberg:** if you do not wish to walk up, you can drive up on the Viennese "Höhenstrasse".

Resistance (see Museums) are to be found in the interior.

1st District, Wipplingerstrasse 8

Am Hof   C 2

In the middle of the largest square in the Inner City is the **Mariensäule** (1664-1667), a column with a statue of the Virgin Mary – she is a memorial of the threat of Swedish troops in the Thirty Years' War. On the site of today's "Länderbank", Heinrich Jasomirgott founded the residence of the Austrian dukes, the Babenbergs (from 1150 to 1220) in front of which was Vienna's oldest tiltyard. The **Church of the Nine Choirs of Angels (Kirche "Zu den neun Chören der Engel")** has a musical terrace next to the beautiful Baroque facade from the 17th century. This is where Pope Pius VI gave his blessing during his visit on Easter Sunday 1782. To the left of the church is the Baroque **Palais Collalto** (No. 13) by Lukas von Hildebrandt. Other Baroque buildings include the **Viennese Fire Brigade Museum** and the **Urbanihaus** (No. 12), house number 8 is one of the oldest in the City (16th century). At the far end of the square is the Baroque facade of the former **Civil Arsenal (Bürgerliches Zeughaus),** today the headquarters of the fire brigade; in the adjoining building (No. 9) Roman ruins can be viewed.

1st District

21

(Annakirche)
Church of St. Anne   C 3

The originally Gothic church in the Anna lane (Annagasse) was redesigned in the Baroque style by the Jesuits around 1715. Daniel Gran painted the ceiling frescoes and the painting on the high altar (around 1717). A wood carving of "St. Anne with Mary and the Child Jesus" is attributed to the Nuremberg artist Veit Stoss (around 1505). The church's most precious relic is a hand of St. Anne that is exhibited on 26th July, the feast of the saint.

1st District, Annagasse

Augarten

At the end of the 17th century an imperial pleasure garden was laid out in an area previously inundated by the Danube. In 1712 the landscape gardener Jean Trehet added

The Vienna Boys' Choir

The tradition of the world-famous choir with the clear ring of boys' voices goes back to the year 1498 when Emporer Maximilian I founded the Court Orchestra. The cost of training and educating the 16 to 20 "orchestra boys" was met by the imperial privy purse. Famous members of the Boys' Choir include Joseph Haydn, his brother Michael and Franz Schubert.

In 1924 the ensemble was refounded as the "Vienna Boys' Choir" (Wiener Sängerknaben). A society financially supports this old Viennese institution. The boys are admitted between the ages of 6 and 10, they live in the home in the Augarten Palace and attend a public school. After their voices break the boys can stay till they have finished school and then move to the "Mutantenheim" in the Josephsstöckl. The repertoire of this first-class boys choir ranges from old medieval madrigals to tricky contemporary vocal music. The boys' main job (they now make up four choirs of 22 to 24 boys each) is to sing at the church service' in the Hofburgkapelle (Palace Chapel) on Sundays at 9:15 am (except July to mid-September). Apart from that they have numerous commitments in the Concert Hall, at the Opera and at the studio for recordings. One of the four choirs is usually on a concert tour, one of their many tours all over the world – as Austria's musical ambassador.

Tel. 2163942

a French touch to the park. Joseph II opened the garden to the public – as a "place of pleasure dedicated to all people".

From 1704-1706 Emperor Joseph I had the **"Gartensaal" (summer pavilion)** built in place of the garden palace that had been destroyed by the Turks. As from 1782 Joseph II's "morning concerts", conducted by Mozart and later by Beethoven, took place here. Today the famous Augarten Porcelain Manufacture is installed in this building.

The **Augarten Palace** has housed the boarding school of the Vienna Boys' Choir since 1948. It was built at the close of the 17th century in Johann Bernhard Fischer von Erlach's Baroque style. Joseph II bought it, but had the **"Josephsstöckl"**, a small pavilion, built for himself to which he sometimes retreated.

2nd District, Obere Augartenstrasse 2-3

(Augustinerkirche)
Augustinian Church   C 3

After having been redecorated in the Baroque style, this towering Gothic hall church (1330-1339) of the Augustinian order was returned to the Gothic. It was in this church, adjacent to the Hofburg, that the crowning ceremonies and royal weddings took place: the wedding of Archduchess Maria Louise and Napoleon (who had someone else represent him), that of Emperor Franz Joseph and Elisabeth of Bavaria and of crown prince Rudolph and Stephanie of Belgium.

A principal work in classical sculpture is the tomb for Archduchess Marie Christine (Maria Theresia's favourite daughter) by Antonio

Canova (1805).

The **"Herzgruft" (Heart Crypt)** is a somewhat macabre place: this crypt holds 54 silver urns with the hearts of the Habsburgs (the bodies are in the Capuchin Monastery Church and the organs in St. Stephen's Cathedral).

1st District, Augustinerstrasse 3;
Guided tours by appointment; Tel. 5337099

Ballhausplatz   B 3

The name refers to a former "Ballhaus" opposite the Secret Chancellory where a kind of indoor tennis was played in the middle of the 18th century. The name "Ballhausplatz" is inextricably linked with 250 years of Austrian politics that were "brewed" in the Secret Chancellory, today's **Federal Chancellory** (seat of the Austrian Federal Government and the Foreign Ministry). The building was constructed from 1717 to 1719 according to plans by Lukas von Hildebrandt and extended in 1766 by Nikolaus Pacassi.

1st District

Belvedere   D 5

Within the space of 10 years Lukas von Hildebrandt created his most significant work, one of the largest palaces, including the palace grounds, in the Baroque style in Europe. He designed it for Eugene of Savoy, the victorious Austrian general under three emperors. Between 1714 and 1716 the Prince's summer residence, the Lower Belvedere, was built. Its rather plain exterior is made up for by the display of splendour in the interior (Marble Hall, Marble Gallery, Garden Room).

View of the park of the Upper Belvedere

Hildebrandt then added a final touch to complete the splendour: he had a pleasure palace built on the hilltop. It was to serve as a place for entertainment and for official and social events. The wonderful view from the Upper Palace later led to its name: Belvedere, meaning "beautiful view".

The symmetrical park, laid out in the French style, gently rising in terraces, bridges the distance of 1 km between the palaces.

The Lower Belvedere has housed the **Austrian Museum of Baroque Art** and the **Museum of Medieval Art** since 1923, the Upper Belvedere is home to the **Austrian Gallery, featuring Austrian and international art of the 19th and 20th Centuries** *(see Museums)*.

Upper Belvedere: 3rd District, Prinz-Eugen-Strasse 27; Tel. 79557-134

Lower Belvedere: 3rd District, Rennweg 6a
Opening hours: daily, except Mon,
10 am-6 pm

(Ehem. **Böhmische Hofkanzlei**) **Former Chancellory of Bohemia** C 2

With this building Johann Bernhard Fischer von Erlach succeeded in achieving a symbiosis of French and Italian high Baroque (1710-1714).
After being badly damaged during the War, it was adapted between 1946 and 1951 to create a pedestrian passage to Wipplingerstrasse. Today the building is the seat of the Constitutional and Administrative Courts.

1st District, Wipplingerstrasse 7

(Börse) Stock Exchange C 1

Theophil van Hansen was the architect of this historic Renaissance building (1874-1877) for the stock exchange. It was founded in 1771 and modelled after its Paris counterpart. After the main stock exchange hall was destroyed in a fire in 1956, the interior and the court-yard were modernized though the lovely facade still stands.

1st District, Schottenring 16

(Botanischer Garten)
Botanic Gardens

Maria Theresia's herbal garden, laid out in 1754 for medicinal purposes, was the forerunner of the Botanic Gardens. She gave her garden to the university in 1757. In its function as part of the Department of Botany at the University of Vienna, the succulents, the cultivation of orchids and a collection of Australian plants are of particular interest. To the south of the Botanic Gardens are the Alpine Gardens.

3rd District, Mechelgasse 2
Opening hours: April till Oct daily from 9 am till dusk

Burggarten   BC 3

Emperor Franz I had a small park laid out, now between the Burgring and the wing of the new Hofburg, on the site of the city ramparts that had been blown up by Napoleon in 1809. The park was first reserved

Mozart Monument

for the royal family but has been accessible to the public since 1919. The memorials to be seen here are **Abraham a Santa Clara** (1644-1709, preacher in Vienna during the 2nd Turkish siege), **Emperor Franz I** (the oldest equestrian statue in Vienna by Balthasar Moll, 1781), **Wolfgang Amadeus Mozart** (marble statue by Victor Tilgner) and **Emperor Franz Joseph I** (bronze statue).

1st District, Opernring

National Theater: the foremost German-language theater

(Burgtheater) National Theatre B 2

One of the German language's greatest stages was bestowed with an appropriate setting when the Burgtheater was built from 1874 to 1888 by Karl von Hasenauer and Gottfried Semper on the Ringstrasse. The historic Renaissance facade is structured by reliefs, the "Bacchic Revel" by Rudolf Weyr and the busts of famous playwrights by Victor Tilgner and Karl Kundmann. The interior embodies the style of the French Baroque. Frescoes by Gustav and Ernst Klimt, and by Franz Matsch decorate the grand stairways.

After being partially destroyed in World War II, a spectacular reopening with Franz Grillparzer's drama "King Ottokar, His Rise and Fall" took place on 15th October 1955.

1st District, Dr.-Karl-Lueger-Ring 2

(Deutschordenskirche) Church of the Teutonic Knights D 3

The Teutonic Order, called to Vienna in the 14th century, founded a chapter house within which the church was erected. The church owes its present form to Anton Erhard Martinelli (1720-1725).

The **Treasury of the Teutonic Order** including the art gallery of Archduke Maximilian III is on display in four rooms.

Opening hours: Mon, Thurs, Sat 10-noon, Wed, Fri, Sat 3-5 pm; Tel. 5121065

(Dominikanerkirche) Dominican Church Maria Rotonda D 2/3

Since being raised to the status of a Basilica Minor in the year 1927, this church bears the name "Rosary Basilica of St. Maria Rotonda". Today's place of worship dating from 1631/32 – the third structure since it was first consecrated in 1237 – in one of the most significant Early Baroque churches in Vienna. The frescoes by Matthias Rauchmiller in the nave (17th century), the dome frescoes by Franz Geyling (1836) and the high altar painting "Mary, Queen of the Rosary" by Leopold Kupelwieser" (1839, when the Rosary Celebration was proclaimed by Pope Gregory XIII), are all well worth seeing.

1st District, Postgasse 4

(Donaupark) Danube Park

The second largest park in the city was laid out in 1964 on the occasion of the "Vienna International Garden Show". Vienna's tallest structure, the 252-m-high **Danube Tower** offers a wonderful panoramic view of the near and far surroundings which can be enjoyed in the revolving Café Restaurant (at a height of 170 m).

22nd District
Opening hours: daily 10 am-11:30 pm;
Tel. for table reservations in the restaurant 2633572-32

Danube Tower

Dorotheum C 3

In 1787 the pawnbroking office (founded in 1707) relocated to the Convent of St. Dorothy, which had been closed down under Joseph II, hence the name "Dorotheum" (known colloquially as "Aunt Dorothy" or "s'Pfandl").
As space had become too limited the building as it stands today was constructed according to a design by Emil von Förster from 1898-1901 in the Neo-Baroque style. Besides auctions that take place regularly there are four big art auctions here every year in one of the largest pawn brokers and auction houses in the world.

1st District, Dorotheergasse 17; Tel. 51560

(Evangelische Kirchen) Lutheran Churches C 3

After the dissolution of the convent church of the Poor Clares under Joseph II (1582/83 by court architect J. Vivian), a Lutheran Church, Augsburg Confession, was created in 1783 as a consequence of the "Edict of Tolerance". To the right of this church, the oldest Lutheran church in Vienna (Renaissance interior), the Reformed Church (Helvetic Confession) was built by Gottlieb Nigelli between 1783 and 1784; the Neo-Baroque facade was added in 1887.

1st District, Dorotheergasse 16, 18

(Franziskanerkirche) Fransiscan Church of St. Hieronymus D 3

Together with attractive house facades from the 17th and 18th centuries, this Gothic church, already under the influence of the South German Renaissance style, frames the small **Franziskanerplatz (Franciscan Square)** with the **Moses Fountain** (by Johann Martin Fischer, 1798). In the Baroque interior one cannot overlook the very ornate high altar, created by Andrea Pozzo in 1707, with its woodcarving of the Madonna (15th century). The paintings of famous Baroque artists on the side altars such as "St. Capistran Heals a Man Possessed" by Franz Xaver Wagenschön, "Crucifixion" by Carlo Carlone and "St. Francis" by Johann Martin Schmidt are also worth mentioning. The carved Baroque organ by Johann Wöckerl (1643) is the oldest in Vienna.

1st District, Franziskanerplatz

Freyung B 2

The plaza in front of the "Schottenstift" (Scots Abbey) is surrounded by grand palaces from the 17th and 18th centuries: the highly Baroque **Daun-Kinsky Palace** on the north side was created by Lukas von Hildebrandt for the fieldmarshal Daun (1713-1716); to the left is the former **Porcia Palace** from the Renaissance; the **Harrach Palace** opposite was probably built by D. Martinelli around 1700 for Count Harrach; the **Ferstel Palace** is characteristic of the Ringstrasse-style (1856-1860), named after its architect Heinrich Ferstel, where **Café Central**, famous as a meeting place for writers, was reopened in 1986.
In the centre of the square is the **Austria Fountain** by Ludwig Schwanthaler (1846): the allegorical figures personify Austria and the four principal rivers of the

monarchy (Po, Elbe, Vistula and Danube).

1st District, Singerstrasse 7

(Gartenpalais Liechtenstein) Garden Palace Liechtenstein

The prince's summer palace was built between 1698 and 1711 by Domenico Martinelli and richly adorned with sculptures by Giovanni Guiliani and his pupils. Johann Michael Rottmayr created the two staircases in the interior with superb ceiling paintings. The ceiling fresco in the Great Hall is the work of Andrea Pozzo.

In March 2004 the **Liechtenstein Museum** will open here, featuring world-ranking air treasures from the prince's collections (extensive painting collection, sculptures, handsome hunting rifles, fine porcelain etc.).

9th District, Fürstengasse 1;
Opening hours: From March 2004: daily 9 am-8 pm, Tel. 3195767

Graben   C 2/3

What was once the moat (Graben) surrounding the Roman fortress Vindobona was filled in during the Middle Ages, then became the market place and a centre of urban life. Today it is one of the most elegant shopping streets in the city. The Baroque **Plague Column** (Holy Trinity Column), erected by Emperor Leopold I, was begun by Matthias Rauchmiller and, after his death, completed by Johann Bernhard Fischer von Erlach.

1st District

Haas-Haus/House   C 2/3

In the middle of Vienna's historic centre, where the Haas commercial

Haas-House with St. Stephen's Cathedral

premises (19th century, Ringstrasse style) were destroyed during World War II, the architect Hans Hollein erected this extravagant and controversial building: a shopping palace for consumers with discriminating taste. It includes a roof-top café. The glass, stone and metal facade reflects a distorted image of St. Stephen's Cathedral.

1st District, Stephansplatz

Hofburg   BC 3

The Hofburg was the residence of the Habsburgs till the end of the Austro-Hungarian Empire in 1918. Today it is the seat of the Austrian president (the Leopold Tract); the extensive building complex next to it with its 18 tracts, 54 staircases, 19 courtyards and 2,600 rooms houses the "Burgkapelle" (Palace Chapel), the Spanish Riding School, the Austrian National Library as well as a number of exhibitions and museums.

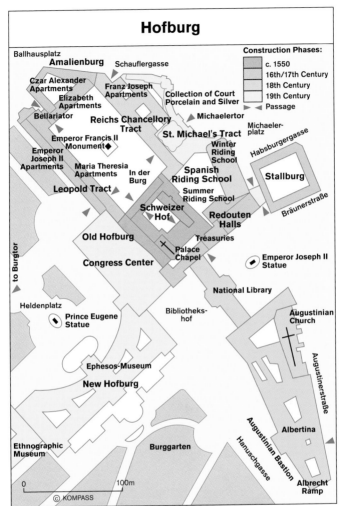

Hofburg

Construction Phases:
- c. 1550
- 16th/17th Century
- 18th Century
- 19th Century
- ► Passage

Ballhausplatz
Amalienburg
Schauflergasse
Czar Alexander Apartments
Franz Joseph Apartments
Collection of Court Porcelain and Silver
Elizabeth Apartments
Bellariator
Reichs Chancellory Tract
Michaelertor
Michaeler-platz
St. Michael's Tract
Emperor Francis II Monument ◆
Emperor Joseph II Apartments
Winter Riding School
Habsburgergasse
Maria Theresia Apartments
In der Burg
Spanish Riding School
Stallburg
Leopold Tract
Summer Riding School
Schweizer Hof
Redouten Halls
Bräunerstraße
Old Hofburg
Treasuries
Palace Chapel
to Burgtor
Congress Center
Emperor Joseph II Statue
National Library
Heldenplatz
Bibliotheks-hof
Augustinian Church
Prince Eugene Statue
Augustinerstraße
Ephesos-Museum
New Hofburg
Augustinian Bastion
Albertina
Ethnographic Museum
Burggarten
Hanuschgasse
Albrecht Ramp

0 ___ 100m

© KOMPASS

The group of 10 buildings of various styles only took on today's form in the course of the centuries after numerous extensions and alterations had been made. The oldest part, the **Schweizerhof (Swiss Court)** or Schweizertrakt (Swiss Tract) where the Swiss Guard had their quarters, was the core of the Babenbergs' "old palace". Ferdinand I had the Renaissance palace with the Swiss gate built (1547-1552). An outdoor stairway leads from here to the **Burgkapelle (Palace Chapel)** that has come down to us in its primarily Gothic style. It dates back to Emperor Frederick III (built from 1447-1449)

29

Hofburg: Neo-Baroque dome on St. Michael's Tract

and was redesigned in the Baroque style in the 17th and 18th centuries; the chapel's interior was returned to the Gothic in 1802. Today the inner courtyard gives access to the ★ **Secular and Ecclesiastical Treasuries (Weltliche und Geistliche Schatzkammer)** *(see Museums)*.

The **Stallburg** is the Renaissance palace built by Emperor Ferdinand I for his son Maximilian in 1558 which was then redesigned to be the court riding stables. The stables for the Lippizaner are here today.

The **Amalienburg** is the former Rudolfsburg. Emperor Maximilian II had it built for his son Rudolf. It has borne this name since the 18th century when the widowed Empress Wilhelmine Amalie moved into the rooms. Empress Elisabeth's apartments and those occupied by Czar Alexander are **on display.**
Under Emperor Leopold I the Baroque connecting tract between the Schweizerhof and the Amalienburg was built (1660-1680). Maria Theresia and her husband Franz Stephan von Lorraine lived in the **Leopold Tract** as did Joseph II whose former study is now used by the Austrian president.

The north-eastern connecting wing between the Schweizerhof and the Amalienburg is the **Reichs Chancellory Tract,** created by the Baroque architects Lukas von Hildebrandt and Joseph Emanuel Fischer von Erlach. The **Imperial Apartments** are on display here, where the **Sisi Museum** will open in April 2004. The renowned stage designer Prof. Rolf Langenfass portrays the "Sisi Myth" in the historic setting of the Hofburg and leaves the popular clichés to give a daring, even critical, view of the famous Austrian empress.

The **Spanish Riding School** performs in the **Winter Riding School.** Joseph Emanuel Fischer von Erlach carried out Emperor Karl VI's orders and designed the hall to be a setting for lavish parties.

The Baroque Court Library that once stood detached, now the **Austrian National Library** (designed by father and son Fischer von Erlach and built from 1723-1726), was connected by the Redouten Tract to the Hofburg. In the central section the 30-metre-high dome with a fresco by Daniel Gran arches above the stately Baroque hall, the magnificent library.

A fire in November 1992 destroyed large portions of the **Redouten Halls**; reconstruction was completed in September 1997. The small hall was authentically reconstructed, because 80% of the structure had been salvaged. The larger hall and the Baroque roof structure above it almost entirely went up in flames. The artistic design of the larger hall was entrusted to the painter Josef Mikl. The former attic now houses a conference hall for approx. 1,000 persons.

Under Franz I (1804) the Classicistic-style extension was added on to the oldest part of the palace, the **Festsaal Tract.** Today the former throne- and ballroom is part of the **Congress Centre.** In place of the Hofburg Theatre, pulled down in 1888, Emperor Franz Joseph I had the **Michaeler Trakt (St. Michael's Tract)** built. It connected the Reichskanzler Trakt (Reichs Chancellory Tract) and the Winter Riding School. Old plans by Joseph Emanuel Fischer von Erlach were used. You enter the Kuppelsaal by passing through the Michaelertor (St. Michael's Gate) from where you can reach the **Silberkammer (Silver Chamber)** and the **rooms open to the public** (Emperor-Franz-Joseph-Apartments).

Karl von Hasenauer and Gottfried Semper planned a huge emperor's forum in the Neo-Baroque style. Emperor Franz Joseph only had one wing, the **New Hofburg,** erected. The open space is filled by the **Heldenplatz** with the Old and the New Hofburg bordering it on two sides. The expanse of this square is dominated only by two equestrian statues – **Prince Eugene of Savoy** and **Archduke Charles,** who defeated Napoleon in the Battle of Aspern. The New Hofburg houses the reading room and the catalogues of the Austrian National Library, the **Globe Museum** and the international **Esperanto Museum** *(see Museums).*

1st District, Michaelerplatz 1, Burgring; Silver Chamber and Imperial Apartments: Opening hours: daily 9 am-5 pm, Tel. 5337570

Guided tours to the Burgkapelle, Jan-end of June and mid-Sept-end of Dec Mon-Thurs 11 am-3 pm, Fri 11 am-1 pm and by prior telephone reservation (groups). Mass in the Hofmusikkapelle with the Vienna Boys' Choir, except July-mid-Sept, Sun 9:15 am. Tickets must be booked in advance! Tel. 5339927-25

Spanish Riding School: Hofburg, Josefsplatz
2: Information on performances under telephone number 5339031

Lippizaner Museum: Reitschulgasse 2,
Opening hours: daily 9 am-6 pm,
Tel. 53410-0

Schmetterlingshaus (Butterfly House),
Burggarten: Opening hours: April to Oct Mon-
Fri 10 am-4:45 pm, Sat, Sun and holidays 10
am-6:15 pm, Nov to March daily 10 am-3:45
pm; Tel. 5338570

Hoher Markt   CD 2

This was the centre of the Roman
civitas Vindobona, the residence of
Emperor Marcus Aurelius. **Roman
ruins** can be viewed inside Hoher
Markt No. 3

Opening hours: Tue-Sun 9 am-12:15 pm,
1-4:30 pm; Tel. 5355606

In the Middle Ages this market
square was the court of law with a
pillary, the scene of countless exe-
cutions. Joseph Emanuel Fischer
von Erlach designed the **Wedding
Fountain** (Joseph's Fountain) in
white marble (1732). During renovation of the insurance building No.
10/11 on the east side of the
square, the artist Franz Matsch put
his idea of a remarkable Jugendstil
clock into effect with the **Ankeruhr.**
Twelve figurines from the history of
Vienna march past as "regents of
the hour" on the flying buttress
(connecting the buildings) above
the lane: Emperor Marcus Aurelius,
Charlemagne, Duke Leopold VI with
Theodora von Byzanz, Walther von
der Vogelweide, King Rudolf I with
his wife Anna, Cathedral architect
Hans Puchsbaum, Emperor Maximilian I, Mayor A. von Liebenberg,
Count Rüdiger von Starhemberg,
Prince Eugene, Maria Theresia with
Emperor Franz I and Joseph Haydn.
The carillon rings out music from
the respective periods as the figures file by at noon every day.
1st District

Hundertwasserhaus

The City of Vienna commissioned
the internationally renowned artist
Friedensreich Hundertwasser, one
of the main critics of the style of
communal residential buildings, to
construct an urban housing complex. Besides the artist's unmistak-
able, ornamental and colourful
style, the complex, built from 1983
to 1985, is marked by the ideas of
committed "Greens": the floors in
the lively, unconventional building
are tilted, the windows are not
symmetrical, the walls are plas-
tered unevenly etc.; there is as lot
of greenery growing on the flat
roofs, crowned with onion-dome
towers, on the terraces and from
the windows – it is not surprising
that this wealth of fantasy attracts
numerous visitors.

3rd District, Kegelgasse/Löwengasse

(Jesuitenkirche, ehemalige Uni-
versitätskirche) Jesuit Church
formerly University Church   D 2

The church, later the University
Church, was founded by Ferdinand
II in rather turbulant years – the
Thirty Years' War and the Counter-
Reformation. The Jesuit pater An-
drea Pozzo designed the High
Baroque nave and the towers, the
high altar and the ceiling frescoes.
1st District, Dr.-Ignaz-Seipel-Platz

Josefsplatz   C 3

Magnificent facades – Baroque to
Classicist – surround the square
which is said to be the most beautiful one in Vienna. The **National Library** with its adjacent wings is
Baroque in style. Franz Anton Zauner created an imposing Classicistic portal (1784) for the **Palla-**

vicini Palace opposite. The **equestrian statue of Emperor Joseph II** (1807) on the square is by the same artist. The plain exterior of the **Pálffy Palace** on the east side dates back to the 16th century.

1st District

(Kapuzinerkirche mit Kaisergruft) Capuchin Church with Imperial Crypt C 3

This church of simple construction, in accordance with the mendicant order, has been the final resting place of the Habsburgs since 1633. To the left of the church is the **Kaisergruft (Imperial Crypt)**, which has been enlarged several times since the 17th century. Here lie 145 members of the Habsburg dynasty (without their organs or hearts). The sarcophagi and coffins, some plain, some artistically decorated, are to be found in the chronologically arranged crypts. Here is also the intricate Rococo twin sarcophagus of Maria Theresia and Franz I by Balthasar Moll (1753).

1st District, Neuer Markt/Tegetthofstrasse
Opening hours: daily 9:30 am-4 pm;
Tel. 5126853-12

Karl Marx Hof

The 1000-metre-long apartment complex with its striking arches, a symbol of "Red Vienna" was built by Karl Ehn. The era of the Social Democratic Party (1919-1934) was famous for its municipal housing complexes.

19th District, Heiligenstädter Strasse 82-92

★ (Karlskirche) Church of St. Charles Borromeo C 5

The Church of St. Charles Borromeo was founded by Emperor Karl VI in 1713, Johann Bernhard Fischer von Erlach began building in 1716 and his son Joseph Emanuel completed this most significant Baroque church in Vienna in 1739. It is even a masterpiece of European Baroque. In 1725 the dome (72 m high, lift available to dome) was completed and decorated with wonderful frescoes by Johann Michael Rottmayr, who also painted the fresco above the organ gallery. Altar-panels such as the "Enlightenment of the Youth of Nain" by Martino Altomonte as well as "Jesus and the Roman Captain" and "Healing of a Palsied Man" by Daniel Gran.

4th District, Karlsplatz

Karlsplatz C 4

This is one of the busiest squares in Vienna as far as traffic is concerned. When it was redesigned in 1977/78, the **Jugendstilpavilions** by Otto Wagner, created for the Stadtbahn (suburban railway), were restored. They compete with the first construction in Viennese Ju-

Baroque perfection: The Church of St. Charles Boromeo by Johann Bernhard Fischer von Erlach

gendstil, the **Secession,** on the west of the square. The southern side of the square is bordered by the magnificent **Church of St. Charles Borromeo** and the Technical University; on the north side is the **Künstlerhaus (Artists' House,** a Neo-Renaissance building, 1865-1868), contemporary art installations and the **Musikvereinsgebäude (Concert Halls),** and on the east side is the Wien Museum Karlsplatz **(Vienna Museum).** The monuments on the lawns of **Resselpark** are memorials to the composers **Johannes Brahms, Josef Ressel** (inventor of ship propellers) and **Josef Madersperger** (inventor of the sewing machine).
1st District

(Maria am Gestade) Church of St. Mary on the Bank   C 1/2

The narrow, Gothic church was built in the 14th century on the site of a Romanesque church, high above a branch of the River Danube. The perforated tracery helm roof is one of the most beautiful Gothic works of art in Austria. Gothic stained-glass windows are still to be found in the choir; two Gothic sandstone figures on the second pillar on the east side of the nave also date back to the 14th century. In a side chapel are the relics of St. Klemens Maria Hofbauer, who has been the patron saint of Vienna since 1914.
1st District, Salvatorgasse 12

(Michaelerkirche) St. Michael's Church   C 3

The former Habsburg parish church, dedicated to St. Michael and originally a late Romanesque buttressed basilica (13th century) was redone in the Gothic style in the 16th century. The narrow Gothic tower is one of the symbols of the Inner City. A Baroque vestibule (1725) and a Classicistic facade (1792) blend in harmoniously with the older part of the church. The Hofburg's **St. Michael's Tract** and the **Loos-House** (Adolf Loos planned this apartment and office complex around 1910/11 in the then revolutionary style of the "New Objectivity") give **St. Michael's Square** its character. During excavation work remains of walls from the Roman Vindobona were discovered. They can be viewed in the middle of the square in the open-air museum, laid out in 1992.

1st District
Tour of the crypts: Mon-Thurs 11 am and 3 pm, Fri 11 am and 1 pm; Tel. 5338000

(Minoritenkirche)
Church of the Friars Minor   B 2

This church, originally built outside the city walls in the 13th century by the Friars Minor, has officially been known as the "Italian National Church Maria Snow" since 1786. The wonderful portal in the northwestern facade of this plain Gothic hall church (14th century) was created by a French master craftsman. In the Classicistic renovated interior visitors can see Martino Altomonte's "Leopold III founds Klosterneuburg", the high altar painting "Maria Snow" by Christoph Unterberger and, in the right-hand aisle, altar paintings by Daniel Gran.

1st District, Minoritenplatz

MuseumsQuartier (MQ)
Vienna   AB 4

See also Museums
The expansive grounds of the former Trade Fair Centre are now home to the new MuseumsQuartier Vienna that was realized after the design by architect Laurids Ortner. It was opened in June 2001. One of the world's ten largest culture complexes, MQ Vienna is a future-ori-entated inner-city culture quarter in the heart of downtown Vienna. It unites Baroque buildings (the spacious imperial stables were built 1719-1725 by Fischer von Erlach, father and son) modern architecture, culture venues of all sizes, a diversity of art, not to mention recreation facilities. Terrace cafés, green oases, bars, shops and bookstores round out the offerings on the 60,000-m^2 areal. The arts spectrum ranges from large museums like the **Leopold Museum** and the **MUMOK (Museum of Modern Art, Leopold Foundation Vienna)** and contemporary exhibition spaces such as **KUNSTHALLE vienna** to **festivals** such as the Vienna Festival. Add to this an international Dance Quarter of the most modern scale, the **Architecture Center Vienna**, **production studios** for new media, **artists' studios** for "artists in residence," exceptional **art and culture facilities especially for children** (ZOOM Children's Museum, Theater House for Children, viennaXtra kids' info), as well as numerous events and festivals such as the renowned V**iennale Film Festival**, the **ImPulsDance Festival**, etc. Even the **Austrian Tobacco Museum** is located here. The complex is open around the clock. The MQ Info & Ticket Center is open daily from 10 am to 7 pm.

7th District, Museumsplatz 1;
Tel. 5235881-1730

MuseumsQuartier, a mecca for art lovers

(Musikvereinsgebäude)
Concert Halls C 4

The "Gesellschaft der Musik-
freunde" (Society of Music Lovers),
founded in 1812, commissioned
the Ringstrasse architect Theophil
van Hansen to design this building
which is alive with Greek Revival
architecture. Countless premieres
with the Vienna Philharmonic Orchestra have taken place in the
"Golden Hall", famous for its
excellent acoustics. The annual
highlight is the New Year's Concert
which is broadcast from here for
television and satellite transmission
to all corners of the earth.

1st District, Dumbastrasse 3/Bösendorfer-
strasse 12

★ Naschmarkt B 4/5

With its tremendous selection of
fresh foods, fruit, vegetables and
exotic specialities, Naschmarkt has
a certain Viennese charm (opening
hours: Mon-Fri 6 am-6:30 pm, Sat
6 am-1 pm). The flea market at the
southern end of the Naschmarkt is
open every Saturday. You can find
everything there from valuable antiques to kitsch and junk.

6th District, Wienzeile

"Naschmarkt"

(Neidhart-Fresken)
Neidhart Frescoes C 2

The oldest secular wall paintings in
the City of Vienna were accidentally
discovered in 1979 during renovation work. They were done around
1400 to decorate a medieval ban-
queting hall. They depict scenes in
the poetry of the minnesinger Neidhart. When redecoration in the
Baroque style took place, they were
partly destroyed and partly smooth-
ed over with plaster.

1st District, Tuchlauben 19
Opening hours: Tue-Sun 9 am-12 pm;
Tel. 5359065

Neuer Markt
with Donner-Fountain C 3

Neuer Markt has been a market
square ever since 1220 (Mehlmarkt
– Flour Market) and was also a
tournament site. Besides the **Capuchin Church** (Kapuzinerkirche) it
is today surrounded by several
buildings that date back to the 18th
century. In the middle of the square
stands the fountain created by the
sculptor Georg Raphael Donner.
Providence, in the centre of the fountain, is surrounded by the allegorical
figures symbolizing the rivers Enns,
Traun, Ybbs and March, sitting on the
fountain edge. The original sculpture
can be seen in the Baroque Museum;
they have been replaced by bronze
replicas.

1st District

(Palais Lobkowitz)
Lobkowitz Palace C 3

This palace was built between
1685 and 1687. Johann Bernhard
Fischer von Erlach later added the
parapet and the main portal. It was
here that Ludwig van Beethoven
first conducted his third symphony,

the "Eroica Symphony" before a private audience in 1803.

1st District, Lobkowitzplatz 1

(Palais Pálffy) Pálffy Palace, Pallavicini Palace

see Josefsplatz

(Palais Rasumofsky) Rasumofsky Palace

The Russian envoy to Vienna and art connoisseur had this palace built by Louis de Montoyer (1806/07). The Grand Hall was very much in demand due to its excellent acoustics – Beethoven's Fifth Symphony premiered here. A fire in 1814 destroyed the entire interior of the palace.

3rd District, Rasumofskygasse 23-25

(Palais Schwarzenberg) Schwarzenberg Palace   D 5

This building, today a hotel and restaurant, was created by Lukas von Hildebrandt around 1704. The interior with the magnificent domed hall and the Baroque gardens were the work of Johann Bernhard Fischer von Erlach from 1720 on. The ceiling fresco in the gallery was created by Daniel Gran.

3rd District, Rennweg 2

(Palais Trautson) Trautson Palace   A 3

Today this building houses the Austrian Ministry of Justice. It is the most important secular structure that the famous Baroque architect, Johann Bernhard Fischer von Erlach, built in Vienna. Maria Theresia took over the building in 1760 to quarter the Imperial Hungarian Guards.

7th District, Museumstrasse 7

(Parlament) Parliament   A 3

Parliament, where the National Assembly and the Federal Council meet

As the crowning achievement of his work performed along Ringstrasse Theophil van Hansen built the Austrian Parliament from 1873 to 1883. The style of a Greek temple is intended to make the imaginary connection with Greece, the cradle of democracy. The triangular gable above the columned entrance hall shows a relief by Edmund Heller, the "Bestowal of the Constitution on the 17 Crown Lands by Emperor Franz Joseph I". Below the ramp is the **fountain** by the sculptor Karl Kundmann (1902) with **Pallas Athene**, the Greek Goddess of Wisdom.

1st District, Dr.-Karl-Renner-Ring 3; Guided tours, except when in session: Mon-Thurs 11 am and 3 pm, Fri 11 am and 1, 2, 3 pm; Mon-Sun groups by prior arrangement; July to mid-Sept Mon-Fri 9, 10, 11 am, 1, 2, 3 pm; Tel. 40110-2570

(Peterskirche) St. Peter's Church   C 2

Vienna's second oldest church is

said to have been founded in the year 792 by Charlemagne. Emperor Leopold I commissioned construction of this Baroque church: a centralized building with an oval floor plan, begun in 1702 by Gabriele Montani and completed by Lukas von Hildebrandt, inspired by St. Peter's in Rome. The two towers, standing at a slight angle on both sides of the dome, were added in 1733. The portal was designed by Andrea Altomonte. In the beautiful interior with gold-ochre stucco work the dome fresco by J. M. Rottmayr is particularly striking. Martino Altomonte painted the high altar panel and the painting "Maria Immaculata" above the tabernacle is the work of Leopold Kupelwieser. There are more altar panels and paintings by M. Altomonte and L. Kupelwieser in the side-chapels.

1st District, Petersplatz

(Piaristenkirche Maria Treu) St. Mary's Church of the Collegium Piarum Scholarum

This church of the holy order of the Patres Scholarum Piarum (Piarists) was begun according to plans by Lukas von Hildebrandt around 1716, but not continued till the middle of the 18th century. With its two high towers (76 m) it is one of the most impressive churches in Vienna. The wonderful frescoes inside are the first masterpieces by Franz Anton Maulbertsch (1752/53). Another painting done by the Baroque artist around 1772 is to be seen in the cruciform chapel.

8th District, Jodok-Fink-Platz

★ Prater

This large park area, stretching for almost 10 km within the municipal area between the Danube and the Danube Canal, was once forest and meadowland. It was first documented around 1162 as the private hunting grounds of the imperial family (name from the Spanish "prado" = meadow).
The main boulevard, lined with chestnut trees and laid out by Ferdinand I in 1537 leads to the "Lusthaus" (pleasure house), a Classicistic pavilion (built in 1782, today a restaurant and coffeehouse). Emperor Joseph II opened these imperial lands to the public in 1766 and they soon became one of the city's most popular recreation areas. The fireworks on the Jesuit meadow were especially popular. Three cafés sprang up on the main boulevard where famous musicians performed: Beethoven, Lanner and the Strauss Brothers, among others. At the exit, near the Praterstern, the first booths appeared and the **"Volksprater"** (people's prater) or **"Wurstelprater"** (from "Wurstel" = a clown puppet similar to Punch) began to establish itself. The first Prater ring game by Calafati was played in 1840. The 67-m-high **Giant Ferris Wheel (Riesenrad),** constructed by the Englishman W. B. Bassett, became Vienna's second landmark. While the wheel slowly turns you can enjoy the panorama from one of the fifteen cars. Today there are all kinds of entertainment, roller coasters, ghost trains, amusement arcades, shooting galleries etc. The "Watschenmann" (fairground dummy) is a famous figure. A miniature train with diesel locomotive runs from the Riesenrad through the

Green Prater to the Lusthaus and back. The Giant Ferris Wheel has a new attraction: the "panorama" at the entrance shows the history of the giant wheel (diameter, 61 meters) and of Vienna in nostalgic pictures in ferris wheel cars that parade past their viewers. The Green Prater is the extensive part of the Prater covered by woods and meadows beyond the amusement park.

Opening hours of the Giant Ferris Wheel (Riesenrad): Jan, Feb, Nov and Dec 10 am-8 pm, Mar, Apr and Oct 10 am-10 pm, May-Sept 9 am-midnight; Tel. 7295430

(Rathaus) City Hall   A 2

The new Vienna City Hall – the old one had become too small – was built between 1872 and 1883 by Friedrich von Schmidt in the Neo-Gothic style and modelled after the Gothic city hall in Brussels. The main facade, facing Ringstrasse, is characterized by a middle projection, from which rises a 98-m-high main tower (crowned by the Rathausmann – the "City Hall Man"), and by open arcades and loggias. The Arcade Courtyard (Arkadenhof) is the largest of the seven inner courtyards, the scene of concerts during the Vienna Music Summer (Wiener Musiksommer). In the two-storey conference hall of the district council and (simultaneously) of the provincial government, one is impressed by the magnificent chandelier from 1873 (3.2 tons, 254 lamps), the richly gilded wooden coffered ceiling and a 25-m-long fresco frieze depicting important events from Vienna's history. Two lovely staircas-

Vienna City Hall is crowned by the "Rathausmann"

es lead up to the Great Hall that takes up two storeys. This is where the "Concordia Ball" takes place every summer. The space between City Hall and Ringstrasse is filled by **City Hall Park;** in the middle of the park is the access road, lined with statues of famous personages from the history of the city. Even among the shrubs and beneath the trees, wherever you go you come across memorials to Viennese artists, politicians and scientists.

1st District, Friedrich-Schmidt-Platz 1; Guided tours, except when in session and holidays: Mon, Wed and Fri 1 pm. Groups by prior arrangement. Tel. 52550

Ringstrasse   C 1 – D 4

By razing the city fortifications, room was made for the 4-km-long Ringstrasse which surrounds the historical city centre (1858-1865). In the second half of the 19th century construction of the monumental buildings began. These included the State Opera House (as from 1861), the Museums of Fine Art and Natural History (1872), Parliament and the Government Building on Stubenring, which was completed shortly before the First World War. The typical "Ringstrasse Architectural Style" was historicism, making it possible to have different architetural styles that had developed and were successful throughout the centuries side by side – Classical alongside Gothic, Renaissance or Baroque. These magnificent edifices were built by such architects as Heinrich Ferstel, Theophil van Hansen, Karl von Hasenauer, Eduard van der Null, Friedrich von Schmidt, Gottfried Semper and August von Siccardsburg.

1st District

(Ruprechtskirche)
St. Ruprecht's Church   D 2

Legend has it that this church, the oldest in Vienna, was founded in the 8th century by Bishop Virgil. It was mentioned as the city's parish church around 1161 (St. Stephen's was a daughter church). The nave of this simple Romanesque building dates back to the 11th century; the tower was heightened in the 12th century. The oldest stained glass window (13th century) is to be found in the choir. The Gothic organ gallery with a tracery parapet (1439), a wooden relief, and a picture of St. Ruprecht on the right-hand wall of the choir are all well-worth seeing. The aid of the so-called "Black Madonna" at the Altar of our Lady of Loretto was invoked when the Plague or Turkish siege threatened.

1st District, Ruprechtsplatz

St. Ruprecht's Church: Vienna's oldest church

★ Schönbrunn Palace

The Baroque palace (1996 included in the UNESCO World Heritage List) on the premises of former hunting grounds was the more simple version of the plans that Johann Bernhard Fischer von Erlach presented to Emperor Leopold I. Construction began in 1695 and was completed in 1713 (the idea was to build a palace larger than Versailles on the hill from which the Gloriette now reigns).

Carrousel Room

Maria Theresia had her court architect Nikolaus Pacassi decorate the residence from 1744-1749. Until the monarchy came to an end the three-storey building in the typical "Schönbrunn yellow" was the Habsburgs' residence. After being badly damaged during World War II, the palace was renovated and today the Austrian President receives heads of states and other guests in Schönbrunn. Of the 1441 rooms, 42 are open to the public. Among these are such magnificent and original ones as the Round Chinese Room, the Rosa Room, the Mirror Room, the Small and the Great Gallery, the Blue Drawing Room, the Napoleon Room, the Million's Room, the Tapestry Room and the Ceremonial Hall, to mention only a few.

The **Palace Chapel** (1700) has ceiling frescoes by Daniel Gran and a high altar picture by Paul Troger.

In the **"Wagenburg" (Coach Museum),** the former Winter Riding School, historic coaches and other vehicles that belonged to the imperial family are on display.

The **Rococo Theatre** in the palace (1766/67) is Vienna's oldest remaining theatre. Both Mozart and Haydn gave concerts here.

The grandiose **Palace Park** was laid out by Jean Trehet in severe geo-

Schönbrunn Palace, the most popular of Vienna's attractions

Gloriette

metric forms with trimmed hedges and trees as well as terraces with fountains such as the **"Neptune Fountain"** in the central axis with stone sculptures by F. A. Zauner or the "Schöner Brunnen" ("beautiful fountain", the old spring that gave the palace its name, "schön" = beautiful). At the highest point, the **Gloriette,** a Classicistic pavilion, crowns the Palace Park (1775).
The Gloriette has meanwhile been converted to a coffeehouse with

Dressing and Gymnastic Room

Ceiling paintings by Gregorio Guglielmi in the Great Gallery

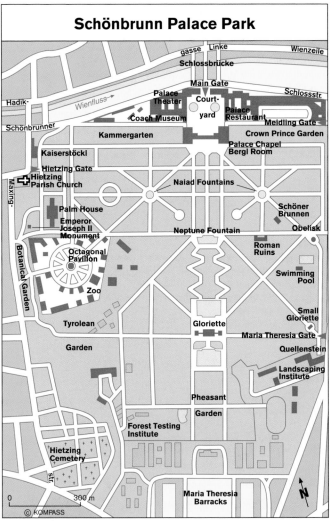

Schönbrunn Palace Park

only minor changes to the structure. The famous view of Vienna can now be admired from inside the glassed-in arches while enjoying a cup of Viennese coffee. Behind the Gloriette is the Pheasant Garden. In the western part of the park is the **Palm House** (Europe's largest greenhouse) and the ★ **Schönbrunn Zoo** (founded 1752, the oldest in the world), next to which is the **Tiroler Garten** (Tyrolean Garden) set up in 1800 by Archduke Johann.

The historic **Sundial House** in the Palace Park shines in new glory af-

Schönbrunn Zoo: baby animals are fun for everyone

ter a complete renovation and now houses the **Desert House** (Wüsten-haus) that gives an impression of the fascinating flora and fauna of this arid habitat. There are numerous botanical rarities to be admired.

13th District, Schönbrunner Schlossstrasse
Opening hours: Rooms open to the public

(only guided tours): Nov-Mar daily 8:30 am-4:30 pm, Apr-June, Sept and Oct daily 8:30 am-5 pm, July and Aug daily 8:30 am-6 pm, Children's tours: Sat, Sun and holidays 10:30 am and 2:30 pm; Tel. 81113-239

Gloriette: Café, daily 9 am-dusk; Tel. 8791311

Irrgarten (Maze): Apr-June and Sept daily 9 am-6 pm, July and Aug daily 9 am-7 pm, Oct daily 9 am-5 pm, Nov 10 am-4 pm; Tel. 81113-239

Palm House and its abundance of exotic plants

Maze in Schönbrunn Park

Palmenhaus (Palm House): May-Sept daily 9:30 am-5:30 pm, Oct-Apr 9:30 am-4:30 pm; Tel. 8775087-406

Schlosspark (Palace Park): 6 am till dusk

Wagenburg (Coach Museum): Apr-Oct daily 9 am-6 pm, Nov-March, daily, except Mon, 10 am-4 pm; Tel. 8773244

Wüstenhaus (Desert House): May-Sept 9 am-6 pm, Oct-Apr 9 am-5 pm; Tel. 8775087

Zoo: daily! Jan, Nov and Dec 9 am-4:30 pm, Feb 9 am-5 pm, March and Oct 9 am-5:30 pm, April 9 am-6 pm, May to Sept 9 am-6:30 pm; Tel. 8779294-0

(Schottenkirche) Scots Church   B 2

After the Schottenstift (Scots Monastery) was founded by Heinrich Jasomirgott in 1155, construction of the church began around 1177. The Irish Benedictine monks were known as "Scots" as this people originally came from Ireland. The church was remodelled in the Gothic style in the 14th and 15th centuries and in the Baroque in the 17th century. Beautiful altar-panels

by Tobias Pock, among others, can be seen here.

The **Schottenstift (Scots Abbey)** is home to a **museum**.

1st District, Freyung 6
Opening hours: Thurs-Sat 10 am-5 pm, Sun and holidays 10:30 am-5 pm; Tel. 53498-600

Schwarzenbergplatz   D 4/5

In the centre of this square stands the **equestrian statue** of Prince Karl von Schwarzenberg, the victorious commander of the Austrian, Prussian and Russian troops against Napoleon at the Battle of the Nations near Leipzig in 1813. (The statue is by Ernst Julius Hähnel). At the southern end of the square is the **high-pressure fountain,** built to commemorate the opening of the First Viennese Aqueduct which provides the city with spring water from the Rax and Schneeberg regions.

3rd District

Secession *see Museums*

(Staatsoper) State Opera House   C 4

The State Opera, one of the world's foremost opera houses, was the first building to be erected along Ringstrasse (1861-1869). August von Siccardsburg and Eduard van der Nüll, the architects of this monumental structure in the style of the French Renaissance, did not live to experience the opening of the new court opera theatre in the year 1869. Harsh criticism of their work (said to look more like a "railway station") drove van der Nüll to suicide; Siccardsburg died shortly thereafter. World War II bombs almost completely destroyed the Opera House – only the ceremonial

World-famous: the Vienna State Opera

staircase, the tea-room and the "Schwind-Foyer" stand as in the original building. The annual Opera Ball on the last Thursday of Fasching, or Carneval, is now a traditional event.

1st District, Opernring 2
Guided tours on request; Tel. 514442613

(Stadtpalais Liechtenstein) Liechtenstein City Palace　B 2

In 1694 the Prince of Liechtenstein acquired this city residence, begun by Domenico Martinelli and completed by Gabriel de Gabrieli. The influence of Roman Baroque architects is obvious. The main portal in Bankgasse was designed by Giovanni Giuliani and is richly decorated with figurines. The Triton Fountain in the courtyard is also by G. Giuliani.

1st District, Minoritenplatz 4/Bankgasse 9

(Stadtpark) City Park　DE 3/4

The largest park in the Inner City was laid out according to plans by Rudolf Sieböck on the former "water glacis"

along the lines of an English garden. Countless statues and busts of famous personalities have been erected in the park through which the Vienna River runs: the "Waltz King" Johann Strauss (1825-1899) by Edmund Hellmer; other composers include Anton Bruckner (1824-1896) by Victor Tilgner, Franz Schubert (1797-1828) by Carl Kundmann, Robert Stolz (1880-1975) by Rudolf Friedl. There are also artists such as Friedrich von Amerling (1803-1887) by Johannes Benk, Hans Canon (1829-1885) by Rudolf Weyr, Hans Makart (1840-1884) by Victor Tilgner and Emil Jakob Schindler (1842-1892) by Edmund Hellmer.

1st District, Parkring

★ (Stephansdom) St. Stephen's Cathedral CD 2/3

St. Stephen's Cathedral (consecrated in 1147) is the seat of the Cardinal-Archbishop and the largest ecclesiastical construction in Vienna. The 137-m-high spire, "Steffl" is the city's most famous landmark. After being

gutted by fire, the original church was rebuilt under Friedrich II, the last of the Babenbergs. The west facade with the Giant Portal (Riesentor) and the Pagans' Towers (Heidentürme) are remnants of the original late Romanesque structure. Under Rudolf IV (Rudolf the Founder) construction of the Gothic nave began (1359), the south tower (Stephen's Tower) was completed in 1433. Work on the north tower by Hans Puchsbaum was discontinued in 1511, the bell tower was added in 1556. In the 19th century the cathedral was thoroughly renovated. However, terrible damage, caused by bombs in 1945, made fundamental restoration work necessary till the year 1961. All the Austrian provinces contributed with financial assistance. One of the most significant late Romanesque masterpieces in Austria is the **Riesentor (Giant Portal)** on the west side, a round arched squinch portal with richly sculptured decorations (around 1240). The High Gothic nave with three aisles and the early Gothic hall choir (there are stained glass windows from 1340-1360 in the centre part), are most impressive with the fan vaults, supported by pillars. Altars, most of which are Baroque, have been set up against the pillars. Anton Pilgram erected a 4-m-high **pulpit** on one of the pillars, a masterpiece of late Gothic stonemasonry (1514-1515) with the four busts of the occidental Doctors of the Church (Ambrosius, Hieronymus, Pope Gregory and Augustinus); at the base of the pulpit the artist portrayed himself as a "Fenstergucker" (peeping out of a window). Directly adjacent to the pulpit is the **"Servant Madonna" ("Dienstbotenmadonna")** an early Gothic statue of the Virgin Mary dating back to 1320.

The **"Pötscher Madonna"** has been held in particular reverence. It stands under a canopy in the right-hand nave next to the Singer Door.
To the right of the high altar is the **imperial tomb of Emperor Frederick III** († 1493), a sight well worth seeing. It is the most magnificent tomb in the Gothic style, created by Niclas Gerhaert van Leyden, with the figure of the emperor chiselled into the red marble memorial slab. In the high choir with the Baroque choir stalls, the black marble **main altar** by Johann Jakob Pock (1649-1670) rises up behind the modern "Volksaltar" (altar facing the congregation). The beautiful altar painting, the "Stoning of St. Stephen" and "Maria's Ascension" on the retable were done by Tobias Pock. On the opposite side of the high altar is the **Wiener Neustadt Altar,** an intricately carved winged Gothic altar, donated by Emperor Frederick III, from the Neukloster Church in Wiener Neustadt. In the north tower, stands the original statue, the **"Zahnwehherrgott"** (toothache Lord) (copy on the outside wall of the choir). Next to the entrance to the lift up the north tower (access to the **Pummerin,** the famous bell) another self-portrait of Anton Pilgram can be found on a late Gothic organbase (the organ no longer exists). From the north tower chapel you can descend to the **catacombs,** a ramified underground network of passageways and chambers, used as a charnel house and burial place when the cemetery on Stephansplatz became too small. When (under Joseph II) it was forbidden to use the catacombs, they were emptied and walled up. The **Imperial Crypt,** laid out by Rudolf IV, the Founder, is accessible. Since the middle of the 17th century the internal

Late Gothic pulpit by Cathedral architect Pilgram in the nave

organs of the members of the House of Habsburg have been stored here in copper urns.

1st District, Stephansplatz; Tel. 51552-3767

Guided tours: Mon-Sat 10:30 am and 3 pm, Sun and holidays 3 pm. Evening tours including roof: June-Sept Sat 7 pm

Opening hours:
South tower (343 steps to the Türmerstube at a height of 72 m), daily 9 am-5:30 pm

North tower (lift to Pummerin): April to Oct 9 am-5:30 pm, Nov to March 8:30 am-5 pm

Catacombs (only guided tours): Mon-Sat 10-11:30 am and 1:30-4:30 pm, Sun and holidays 1:30-4:30 pm

Stephansplatz was a cemetery till 1732 – many memorial sabs are now to be found on the outside wall of the cathedral. When the underground railway was being built, the foundation walls of the former **St. Virgil's Chapel** were discovered.

Opening hours: Tue-Sun 10 am-12:15 pm and 1-4:30 pm

(Synagoge) Synagogue   D 2

Thanks to its hidden location in the courtyard of the Israelite Community, this was the only one of 94 Viennese synagogues that survived the destruction of the Jewish temples in 1938.
The elliptical central plan (1825-1826) is a masterpiece by Joseph Kornhäusel, who also designed the interior.

1st District, Seitenstettengasse 2-4

(Universität) University   AB 1/2

The University, built in the Neo-Renaissance style according to plans by Heinrich Ferstel, was opened on the former parade grounds of the Imperial army.

1st District, Dr.-Karl-Lueger-Ring 1

(Volksgarten)
Public Gardens
B 2/3

The Public Gardens were laid out for the Viennese people in 1820. They are between the Hofburg and the Burgtheater where the castle bastion, blown up by the French, once stood. The classicistic **Theseus Temple** by Peter Nobile is in the grounds of the Public Gardens. It was built in 1823 for a Theseus statue by A. Canova (since 1890 in the Museum of Fine Art). The following memorials are also in the Public Gardens: The **Empress Elisabeth Memorial** (1837-1898) by Hans Bitterlich, the memorial to the most significant Austrian playwright **Franz Grillparzer** (1791-1872) by Karl Kundmann and Rudolf Weyr and a memorial to **Julius Raab** (1891-1964), Austrian federal chancellor at the time of the Austrian "Staatsvertrag" (international treaty with the occupying powers, signed in 1955) by Toni Schneider-Manzell and Clemens Holzmeister.

1st District, Dr.-Karl-Renner-Ring

(Votivkirche) Votive Church AB 1

When in 1853 Emperor Franz Joseph I escaped an assassination attempt, his brother, Archduke Maximilian, later to be Emperor of Mexico, had the Votive Church built. Heinrich Ferstel succeeded in constructing one of the finest examples of historic architecture, taking French Gothic cathedrals as a model. the church, consecrated to "Christ the Saviour" in 1879, contains the Renaissance tomb of Graf Niklas Salm (1530-1533) as well as the carved Antwerp Altar (15th century) in a side chapel, both well worth seeing.

9th District, Rooseveltplatz

(Zentralfriedhof)
Central Cemetery

The largest cemetery in Vienna, almost resembling a park and criss-crossed with avenues, was opened in 1874. From the main gate (gate II) an avenue leads to the graves of honour of famous persons from the arts, sciences and political life and to the tomb of the Austrian presidents. The **Dr. Karl Lueger Memorial Church** (funeral church) is one of the most significant Jugendstil structures (the plans are by Max Hegele). It was consecrated in 1910.

11th District, Simmeringer Hauptstrasse 234

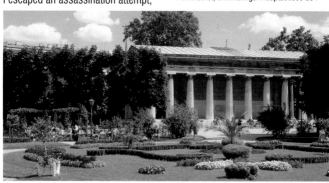

Theseus Temple in the Public Garden (Volksgarten)

WALKING TOURS IN THE CITY

Sketch of tour – see inside flap of booklet

The 1st District alone, the Inner City, possesses a wealth of art and culture; it is rich in history that goes back as far as Roman times. One could spend days just strolling through the streets and lanes, lingering on squares or in parks, there is always something new and interesting to discover. The suggestions made here lead to the best-known and most famous sights and can serve as a kind of framework for further discoveries. The sights in secondary bold print are described in detail in the chapter "Sights to See from A – Z".

A tip for drivers: you should avoid driving in the 1st District because apart from the sparsity of parking garages, which are usually full, you can only park your car in a short-stay parking zone (1½ hours at the most). Try to park in the outer districts and then use public transport (U-Bahn – underground stations in Stephansplatz and Karlsplatz/Opera).

Walking tour through the Medieval Inner City

This walking tour takes about 3 to 4 hours. It takes you to the oldest medieval section of the Inner City where the Babenbergs founded the first duke's court and to the oldest churches.

From **St. Stephen's Cathedral** you turn towards Stock-im-Eisen-Platz which borders on Stephansplatz in the north. Along the glass facade of the **Haas-House** you will reach the **Graben,** one of the most fashionable Inner City shopping streets.

Many street cafés have been set up on this broad street (pedestrian precinct). The buildings mostly date back to the 2nd half of the 19th century, such as the Grabenhof (No. 14/15) or No. 10 (the only preserved store by Otto Wagner). Exceptions are the Baroque palace Bartolotti-Partenfeld from 1720 (No. 11) and the Generalihof (No. 13) one of the first classicistic buildings from 1781 with a shop, designed by Adolf Loos belonging to the Knize company. Loos also designed the subterranean Jugendstil toilets which are worth taking a look at. The Baroque **Holy Trinity Column** (Plague Column) is, however, usually in the centre of most pictures of the Graben. The two fountains in front of and behind the column – the Leopold Fountain and the Joseph Fountain – were decorated with lead figures by Johann Martin Fischer in 1804. You can cast a glance at the Baroque **St. Peter's Church (Peterskirche)** down a side lane on the right. Room was made for St. Peter's in the narrow medieval lanes. Behind the church turn left into the narrow lane to Tuchlauben – in No. 19 you can have a look at the **Neidhart-Frescoes** – then follow Steindlgasse and Seitzergasse to Schulhof. On the corner of Kurrentgasse is the **Clock Museum** of the City of Vienna, in Schulhof No. 2 is the

Holy Trinity Column (Plague Column) on the Graben

Doll and Toy Museum. An alley on the right of the church takes you to the square **Am Hof.** The **Church of the Nine Choirs of Angels (Kirche "Zu den Neun Chören der Engel")** is in an interesting compact row of buildings. After walking along Drahtgasse you reach Judenplatz which, up till the year 1421, the year of the massive persecution of the Jews, was the centre of the ghetto with the rabbi's house and the synagogue. In front of you, the rear of the former **Chancellory of Bohemia (Böhmische Hofkanzlei)** borders on the square. On the main facade in Wipplingerstrasse you can see the coats of arms of Bohemia and Moravia above the magnificent portal. Opposite, on the other side of the street, you pass by the **Old City Hall** and walk on to Salvatorgasse where you have a lovely view of the tall, narrow church **St. Mary on the Bank (Maria am Gestade)** with its filigree Gothic spire. Past the **Salvator Chapel** (the front portal is from the Renaissance period) you reach Marc-Aurel-Strasse. Emperor Marcus Aurelius, who died in the year 180, lived in the Roman camp Vindobona which was situated in the area around **Hoher Markt.** The **Roman excavations** at Hoher Markt prove the significance of this square in those days. Hoher Markt was almost completely destroyed in 1945, only the **Wedding Fountain (Vermählungsbrunnen)** and the building housing the Anker Insurance with the interesting **Anker Clock (Ankeruhr)** escaped damage. After walking along Judengasse with its second-hand shops it is not far to the oldest church in the city, the Romanesque **St. Rup-**

recht's Church (Ruprechtskirche). From the past to the present: now you are in the "Bermuda Triangle" – the quarter around Ruprechtsplatz, Rabensteig, Seitenstettengasse, Salzgries – the main meeting place of the "Vienna scene" with a countless number of pubs and bars and a wide selection of music and cabarets. After passing through Seitenstettengasse, the centre of the Viennese orthodox Jewish community with the **Synagogue,** you arrive at the Greek Church (Byzantie facade by Theophil van Hansen). The neighbouring "Griechenbeisel", an historic inn, already mentioned in the 15th century, attracts your attention because of its picturesque appearance. Visitors, including such celebrities as Mozart, Strauss, Grillparzer, Mark Twain and Albert Einstein, have left their autographs on the walls. Cross Fleischmarkt – the Baroque building No. 15 is the birthplace of the artist Moritz von Schwind – and proceed to Postgasse and the Greek-Catholic St. Barbara's Church from the 17th century. You can see the **Dominican Church (Dominikanerkirche)** from here. Turn into Schönlaterngasse, one of old Vienna's prettiest spots and a popular quarter for "in" pubs and bars. At number 6 there is a replica of the street's namesake "lovely lantern" (schöne Laterne), the Basilisk House (Basiliskenhaus) tells of a legend about a monster, No. 9 is the **Old Forge (Alte Schmiede),** a museum and literary centre. From here you can walk through the large complex of the Holy Cross Court (Heiligenkreuzer Hof) via the tranquil Stiftshof. Past Sonnenfelsgasse you

continue on to Dr.-Ignaz-Seipel-Platz which is beautifully framed by the **Jesuit Church (Jesuitenkirche),** former Jesuit monastery, and the **Academy of Sciences (Old University)**. Proceed along Bäckerstrasse, Essiggasse and Wollzeile where the **Archiepiscopal Palace** and the Zwettlhof (fomer monastery courtyard of the Cistercian monks from the Lower Austrian Monastery Zwettl) houses the **Cathedral and Diocesan Museum.** Now you are almost back to where you started out from. From the nearby Domgasse you can pass the **Figarohaus,** and continue on through Grünangergasse to Singerstrasse. The building on the corner of Singerstrasse is the former Rottal Palace from the 17th century, the Fransiscan Monastery lies opposite, adjacent to the **Franciscan Church.** The Baroque Neupauer-Breuner Palace in the Singerstrasse is noteworthy, the Fähnrichshof on the other side dates back to the Middle Ages. From the adjacent Blutgasse front doors lead into small inner courtyards of the Fähnrichshof. If you walk past the huge complex of the **Chapter House of the Teutonic Knights (Deutschordenshaus)** into which is built the **Church of the Teutonic Knights (Deutschordenskirche)** you reach the end of Singerstrasse and are back in Stock-im-Eisen-Platz. The legendary "Stock im Eisen" (stump in iron) stands on the corner of Kärntner Strasse, in the alcoves of numbers 3-4. First mentioned in 1533, legend has it that every passing journeyman locksmith had to hammer a nail into the tree trunk.

Walking tour through imperial Vienna

A pleasant walk that partly leads you through the pedestrian precinct and partly through parks in the Inner City, this relaxing tour will give you an impression of the 600-year period under the rule of the House of Habsburg. This walking tour takes 2 to 3 hours.

From the **Graben** you turn into Kohlmarkt, one of the best-known main shopping streets of the city. Where once, in the 14th century, the market for firewood and coal stood, a grand street developed in the course of the centuries. The processions during which the people paid tribute to the imperial family began at the Hofburg, along Kohlmarkt and on to St. Stephen's Cathedral via the Graben. Many business people who supplied goods to the court had their shops here, among others the imperial Court confectioner's "Demel", today one of the most expensive

cake shops in Vienna. Kohlmarkt opens out onto **Michaelerplatz** with the arch-shaped Michaelertrakt, the part of the Hofburg added in 1890, on the opposite side. To the right on the corner of Herrengasse you can see the **Loos-House**. Among others, even Emperor Franz Joseph disapproved of the plain exterior which he could see from his windows in the Hofburg. Another part of this backdrop is **St. Michael's Church** (formerly the Imperial Family's parish church) on the east side which interrupts the streets that radiate out from here. When you cross over the square you pass the Roman excavations. Proceed through the magnificent gate, the main entrance to the Hofburg (this is also the way to the guided tours), and you will then be in the inner courtyard (you can get to the **Schweizerhof** with the treasure chambers from here) with the Emperor Franz II memorial. On the other side of

Sandstone statues decorate the Hall of the Muses in the Albertina

MuseumsQuartier from the air

the courtyard you can go through to **Heldenplatz** or, if you use the Bellariator, the gate between the Amalien Courtyard (Amalienhof) and the Leopold Tract, you will find yourself directly on **Ballhausplatz.** Turn right, round the **Austrian Federal Chancellory**, which is directly in front of you, and you will see Bruno-Kreisky-Gasse. Walk along this lane till you get to **Minoritenplatz.** The **Church of the Friars Minor (Minoritenkirche)** with its odd pyramid roof (the spire was hit during the Turkish siege) dominates the square. Other buildings such as the state archives, on the other side of the Federal Chancellory, the former **Starhemberg Palace** in the Early Baroque style, the Dietrichstein Palace and the **Liechtenstein City Palace** surround Minoritenplatz. Several Baroque palaces of the old-established Austrian nobility as well as the former seat of the Lower Austrian Government are located in the streets that lead into the square – Regierungsgasse, Landhausgasse, Bankgasse. You can return to Ballhausplatz by walking along Löwelstrasse and enjoy the lovely **Public Gardens (Volksgarten).** At the northern park exit you will be standing in front of the

National Theatre (Burgtheater), one of the greatest structures in **Ringstrasse.** Once on Dr.-Karl-Lueger-Ring you can continue on to the **University** and to the **Votive Church (Votivkirche).** On the other side of this magnificent street (almost 60 m broad) is **City Hall Park (Rathauspark)** where numerous memorials attract your attention. Then comes the huge Gothic facade of the **City Hall (Rathaus).** You can already see the **Parliament** building from the south of the park. The access ramps, lined with

Reminiscent of Gothic cathedrals: the Votive Church

statues of Roman and Greek gods, lead up to an entrance hall reminiscent of a Greek temple. On the other side is Schmerlingplatz with the Palace of Justice. In the small park stands the Memorial to the Republic (1928). The next buildings on the Ringstrasse are the **Museum of Natural History (Naturhistorisches Museum)** and its mirror image the **Museum of Fine Art (Kunsthistorisches Museum).** On Maria-Theresien-Platz in between stands the memorial to Maria Theresia, the only Austrian empress (by Kaspar von Zumbusch, 1888), surrounded by her field marshals. Behind the square you can see the long facade of the new **MuseumsQuartier Vienna.** If you walk through the Babenberg Arcade, you will reach the other side of Burgring where the Outer Palace Gate (Äusseres Burgtor) and the New Hofburg border on Heldenplatz. You can stroll through the adjacent **Palace Garden (Burggarten)** and then walk on to **Albertinaplatz.** The Albertina building rises up above the Albrecht ramp, to the right is the vast Hanuschhof. Streets and lanes branch out from here in all directions: Augustinerstrasse to **Josefsplatz,** Operngasse to Opernring. Follow Philharmonikerstrasse, past the famous **Hotel Sacher,** to Kärntner Strasse. This elegant shopping street with its street cafés, coming to an end at **Karlsplatz** (heading out of the centre), brings us (heading downtown) back to Stephansplatz. Handelsstrasse, leading south, was mentioned as early as 1257 in a document as Strata Carinthianorum and was a connection to the bordering Duchy Karantania. In Annagasse, branching off

to the right, is the **Church of St. Anne (Annakirche),** well worth a visit. The buildings in Kärntner Strasse mostly date back to the 18th century, an exception is the Church of St. John the Baptist (Malteserkirche) on the right hand side of the street. The Gothic structure has a classicistic facade and a remarkable high altarpiece "Baptism of Christ" by Tobias Pock

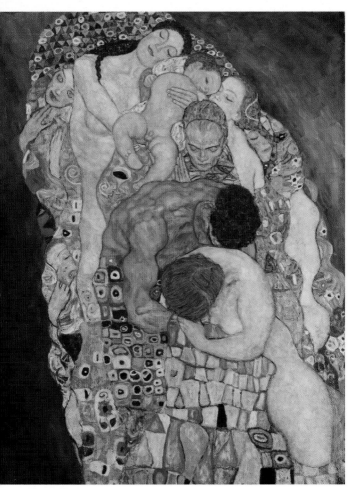

"Death and Life" by Gustav Klimt, Leopold Museum. Vienna's greatest Jugendstil painter used decoration as a means of expression.

(mid 17th century). It is not far to **Neuer Markt** through the side streets on the left. At the southwest end of this square lies the **Capuchin Church (Kapuziner-kirche)** with the Imperial Crypt. You can return to Stephansplatz or Graben, either through the busy Kärntner Strasse or through one of the side streets.

MUSEUMS, EXHIBITIONS, MEMORIALS

The municipal museums are open free of charge Fridays until noon, and the federal museums are free on the first Sunday of every month. For information on other museums, please consult the museum brochure, published by the Vienna Tourist Office (Wien Tourismus). **Pay less with the Vienna Card.** Vienna becomes even more attractive for you. Get on and off the U-Bahn, bus and streetcar as you like (for 72 hours). Enjoy reductions on admission to attractions and museums and many other advantages. The Vienna Card is obtainable from your Vienna hotel, at the tourist information points and wherever tickets for Vienna public transportation are sold.

The letter-number code refers to the coordinates on the city map (inside the front flap of this booklet).

(Akademie der bildenden Künste, Gemäldegalerie) Academy of Fine Arts, Painting Gallery   B 4

1st District, Schillerplatz 3;
Tel. 58816-225
Opening hours: Tue-Sun and holidays
10 am-4pm
The Academy of Fine Arts – the oldest art academy in the German-speaking world, founded in 1692 – moved to the Neo-Renaissance building, erected by Theophil van Hansen in 1876. The ceiling painting "The Fall of the Titans" by Anselm Feuerbach is worth taking a look at.
The **Painting Gallery** has an impressive collection of masterpieces from the 14th century onwards: famous Dutch, Flemish and German artists (Bosch, Cranach, Rubens, van Dyck, Rembrandt), Austrian and Italian masters of the Baroque (Gran, Maulbertsch, Kremser Schmidt, Tiepolo, Guardi), of the Biedermeier period (Waldmüller) and of modern art (Boeckl, Wotruba, Hundertwasser). The world's largest collection of medieval building plans is in the **Copperplate Gallery,** where you will also find 30,000 drawings and prints – hand drawings by Albrecht Dürer and Paul Troger, watercolour paintings by Moritz M. Daffinger, nature studies by Friedrich Gauermann, prints by German Romantics.

Albertina   C 3

1st District, Albertinaplatz 1;
Tel. 53483-0
Opening hours: daily 10 am-6 pm,
Wed 10 am-9 pm
The largest and most significant graphics collection in the world, from the Renaissance to the present, with about 44,000 drawings and aquarelles as well as 1.5 million engravings, etchings and lithographs has its origin in the collections of Duke Albert von Sachsen-Teschen and Prince Eugene of Savoy. It was founded in 1776. Some of the most

Albertina: "Hare" by Albrecht Dürer

famous artists – from many countries and schools – include Albrecht Dürer, Leonardo da Vinci, Peter Paul Rubens, Rembrandt, Raffael and Michelangelo. Don't miss the magnificent Habsburg rooms of state.

(Alte Backstube) Old Bakeshop

8th District, Lange Gasse 34; Tel. 4061101
Opening hours: Tue-Sat 9 am till midnight, Sun 3 pm till midnight, closed mid July to end of August.
Craft and customs of the baker's guild are exhibited in the former bakery. An old Vienna-style café and restaurant add a cosy (gemütlich) atmosphere.

(Alte Schmiede) Old Forge   D 2

1st District, Schönlaterngasse 9; Tel. 5128329
Opening hours: Mon-Fri 10 am-3 pm and by prior arrangement.
Also at the same address is the Literary Quarter, holding readings and concerts.

(Alt-Wiener Schnapsmuseum) Old Vienna Snapps Museum

12th District, Wilhelmstrasse 19; Tel. 8157300
Opening hours: daily 9:30 am-7 pm. Min. 10 persons by prior arrangement.

Aspern 1809 Museum

22nd District, Asperner Heldenplatz 9; Tel. 2808276
Opening hours: Sun 10 am-noon
This little museum is dedicated to the memorable Battle of Aspern (1809), when Napoleon's army was successfully defeated for the first time by the Austrians under Archduke Karl.

Atelier Augarten

2nd District, Scherzergasse 1a; Tel. 79557-134

Gustinus Ambrosi Museum, sculpture garden.
Opening hours: daily, except Mon, 10 am-6 pm

(Österreichisches Barock-museum) Austrian Museum of Baroque Art   D 5

Lower Belvedere, 3rd District, Rennweg 6a; Tel. 79557-134
Opening hours: Tue-Sun 10 am-6 pm
Masterpieces of the Austrian Baroque are on display in the magnificent rooms and halls of the Lower Belvedere: paintings by Martino Altomonte, Paul Troger, Franz Anton Maulbertsch and Kremser Schmidt, sculptures by Johann Michael Rottmayr, Georg Raphael Donner and Franz Xaver Messerschmid.
The **Museum of Medieval Art** in the Orangerie features leading works in sculpture and panel painting from the 12th to the early 16th centuries.

(Bauernfeld-Erinnerungsraum) Bauernfeld Memorial Room

19th District, Döblinger Hauptstrasse 96, Villa Wertheimstein; Tel. 3686546
Opening hours: Sat 3:30-6 pm, Sun 10 am-noon
In the noble residential building of the Biedermeier building several rooms have been set up as a museum to the poets Eduard von Bauernfeld and Ferdinand von Saar.

(Beethoven Gedenkstätten) Beethoven Memorials, Pasqualatihaus   B 2

1st District, Mölker Bastei 8; Tel. 5358905
Opening hours: Tue-Sun 9 am-12:15 pm and 1-4:30 pm
Beethoven lived here at various times between 1804 and 1815 where he composed his symphonies Nos. 4, 5, and 7 and the opera "Fidelio".

Heiligenstadt Testament House

19th District, Probusgasse 6;
Tel. 3705408
Opening hours: Tue-Sun 9 am-12:15
pm and 1-4:30 pm

Eroica House

19th District, Döblinger Hauptstrasse
92; Tel. 3691424
Opening hours: Tue-Sun 9 am-12:15
pm and 1-4:30 pm

(Bestattungsmuseum)
Mortuary Museum

4th District, Goldeggasse 19;
Tel. 50195-4227
Opening hours: by prior arrangement
only
This singularly strange museum has
exhibits documenting a typically Viennese cult of death.

(Bezirksmuseen)
District Museums

In each of Vienna's 23 districts there
is a museum relating to that particular
part of the city.
Innere Stadt
1st District, Wipplingerstrasse 8;
Tel. 53436-01127
Opening hours: Wed and Fri 3-5 pm
Leopoldstadt
2nd District, Karmelitergasse 9;
Tel. 21106-02127
Opening hours: Wed 5:30-7 pm,
Sat 2:30-5 pm, Sun 10-noon
Landstrasse
3rd District, Sechskrügelgasse 11;
Tel. 71134-03127
Opening hours: Wed 4-6 pm,
Sun 10-noon
Wieden
4th District, Klagbaumgasse 4;
Tel. 5817811
Opening hours: Sun 10-noon
Margareten
5th District, Schönbrunner Strasse
54; Tel. 54634-05127
Opening hours: Thurs 4-6 pm

Mariahilf
6th District, Mollardgasse 8;
Tel. 5867868
Opening hours: Thurs and Sun 10-
noon, closed in August
Neubau
7th District, Stiftgasse 8;
Tel. 5245052
Opening hours: Thurs 6-8 pm,
Sat 3-5 pm
Josefstadt
8th District, Schmidgasse 18;
Tel. 4036415
Opening hours: Wed 6-8 pm,
Sun 10-noon
with **Stefan Zweig Archives**
(Fri noon-2 pm) and **Friedrich
Hebbel Memorial**
Alsergrund
9th District, Währinger Strasse 43;
Tel. 40034-09127
Opening hours: Wed 9-11 am,
Sun 10-noon
with **Erich Fried** and **Doderer Memo-
rial** and Alsergrund Gallery
Favoriten
10th District, Ada-Christen-Gasse 2c;
Tel. 6898193
Opening hours: Thurs 5-8 pm only on
schooldays
Simmering
11th District, Enkplatz 2;
Tel. 74034-11127
Opening hours: Fri 10-noon and
3-5 pm, Sun 10-noon
Meidling
12th District, Längenfeldgasse 13-
15; Tel. 8176598
Opening hours: Wed 10-noon and 4-
6 pm, Sun 10-noon
with **Meidling Gallery**
Hietzing
13th District, Am Platz 2;
Tel. 8777688
Opening hours: Wed 9-noon and 2-6
pm, Sat 2-5 pm and Sun 9:30-noon
Penzing
14th District, Penzinger Strasse 59;
Tel. 8972852

Opening hours: Wed 5-7 pm,
Sun 10-noon
with **Heinz Conrad Memorial**
Rudolfsheim-Fünfhaus
15th District, Rosinagasse 4;
Tel. 89134-15127
Opening hours: Fri 3:30-5:30 pm
Ottakring
16th District, Richard-Wagner-Platz
19b; Tel. 49196-127
Opening hours: Sun 10-noon
Hernals
17th District, Hernalser Hauptstrasse
72-74 (Bank Austria);
Tel. 4034338 + 4818375
Opening hours: Mon 4-8 pm and
every 1st and 3rd Sunday in each
month 10-noon (guided tours only by
prior arrangement)
Währing
18th District, Währinger Strasse 124;
Tel. 47634-18127
Opening hours: Thurs 6-8 pm,
Sun 10-noon
Döbling
19th District, Döblinger Hauptstrasse
96; Tel. 3686546
Opening hours: Sat 3:30-6 pm,
Sun 10-noon
with **Museum of Viniculture**
Brigittenau
20th District, Dresdner Strasse 79;
Tel. 3305068
Opening hours: Thurs 5-7 pm,
Sun 10-noon
Floridsdorf
21th District, Prager Strasse 33;
Tel. 2705194
Opening hours: Tue 3-7 pm, Sat 9:30
am-12:30 pm
with Mauthnerschlössl Gallery
Donaustadt
22nd District, Kagraner Platz 53-54;
Tel. 2032126
Opening hours: Wed 5-7 pm,
Sun and public holidays 10-noon
Liesing
23rd District, Canavesegasse 24;
Tel. 8698896

Opening hours: Wed, Sat 9-noon,
Sun 10-noon

Circus and Clown Museum   D 1
2nd District, Karmelitergasse 9;
Tel. 21106-02127
Opening hours: Wed 5:30-7 pm, Sat
2:30-5 pm, Sun 10-noon

Salvador **Dalí Exhibit**   C 3
1st District, Josefsplatz 5;
Tel. 5122549
Opening hours: daily 10 am-6 pm

Demel- and Marzipan
Museum   C 2
1st District, Kohlmarkt 14;
Tel. 5351717
Opening hours: Thurs, Fri 11 am-4
pm, Sat, Sun 11 am-5 pm

(Dokumentationsarchiv des
Österreichischen Widerstandes)
Archives of the Austrian
Resistance   C 2
1st District, Wipplingerstrasse 8 (Old
City Hall); Tel. 53436-90319
Opening hours: Mon-Thurs 9 am-5
pm (by prior arrangement)

(Erzbischöfliches **Dom-**
und Diözesanmuseum)
Archiepiscopal **Cathedral**
and Diocesan Museum   D 2
1st District, Stephansplatz 6, pas-
sageway; Tel. 51552-3560
Opening hours: Tue-Sat 10 am-5 pm
Sacred art from the early Middle Age
up to the present, including precious
pieces from St. Stepen's Cathedral,
Gothic panel paintings and sculptures.

(Ephesosmuseum) Museum of
Ephesian Sculpture   B 3
1st District, Neue Burg, Heldenplatz;
Tel. 52524-0
Opening hours: daily, except Tue, 10
am-6 pm

Unique finds from excavations by the Austrian Archeological Institute are on display here. The exhibits were found in Ephesus, the ancient trading city in Asia Minor in late Hellenistic-Roman days. The most famous pieces are the bronze statue of an athlete (4th century BC), the frieze from the Parthian monument (around 161-165), and parts of an altar from the Artemis shrine (4th century BC).

Esperanto Museum   B 3

1st District, Hofburg, Michaelertor; Tel. 5355145
Opening hours: Mon, Fri 10 am-4 pm, Wed 10 am-6 pm (closed on public holidays)

(Feuerwehrmuseum) Fire Brigade Museum   C 2

1st District, Am Hof 7; Tel. 53199
Opening hours: Sun, holidays 9 am-noon and by prior arrangement

(Fiakermuseum) Hackney Cab Museum

17th District, Veronikagasse 12; Tel. 40106-0
Opening hours: every 1first Wed in each month 10-noon

(Österr. Filmmuseum) Austrian Film Museum   C 3

1st District, Albertinaplatz 1 (Albertina); Tel. 5337054
Showings of international film classics, retrospectives and avant-garde films; Oct-June, several times daily.

(Foltermuseum) Torture Museum

6th District, Fritz-Grünbaum-Platz 1; Tel. 5857185
Opening hours: daily 10 am-6 pm

Sigmund Freud Museum   B 1

9th District, Berggasse 19; Tel. 3191596

Sigmund Freud Museum

Opening hours: Oct-June daily 9 am-5 pm, July-Sept daily 9 am-6 pm; guided tours by prior arrangement. The founder of psychoanalysis lived in this house, built in 1889, from 1891 to 1938, when he then emigrated to London. Part of the 15-room apartment (the rooms of his practice, preserved in their original state, the waiting room and his study) was converted into a museum by the Sigmund Freud Society.

Ernst Fuchs Private Museum

14th District, Hüttelbergstrasse 26, Otto-Wagner-Villa; Tel. 9148575
Opening hours: Mon-Fri 10 am-5 pm (Sat and Sun by prior arrangement)

Otto-Wagner-Villa

Österreichische **Galerie/Belvedere**
Austrian **Gallery/Belvedere**

Upper Belvedere, 3rd District, Prinz-Eugen-Strasse 27;
Tel. 79557-134
Opening hours: Tue-Sun 10 am-6 pm
All the famous Austrian artists and sculptors are represented here. The first floor begins with the 19th century: from the landscape paintings of the Romantics (Moritz von Schwind, Friedrich Gauermann, Adalbert Stifter) to the Biedermeier period (cross-section of the works of the most famous Biedermeier artist Ferdinand Georg Waldmüller, Veduten Rudolf von Alts as well as portraits by Friedrich von Amerling) and historism (Hans Makart). The second floor continues with the 20th century: Gustav Klimt, Egon Schiele and Oskar Kokoschka.

(Österreichisches **Gartenbaumuseum) Austrian Museum of Horticulture**

22nd District, Donizettiweg 29;
Tel. 2032113
Opening hours: 1st Thurs of every month, 10 am-6 pm and by prior arrangement.

(**Gedenkstätte für die Opfer des öster. Freiheitskampfes**) **Memorial for the Victims of the Austrian Fight for Freedom** CD 1

1st District, Salztorgasse 6;
Tel. 53436-90319
Opening hours: Mon 2-5 pm, Thurs, Fri 9 am-noon and 2-5 pm, by prior arrangement.

Geymüller Schlössl Palace

18th District, Khevenhüller Strasse 2;
Tel. 71136-298
Viewings only by prior telephone arrangement.
The palace, constructed in 1808, houses the "Sobek Collection": Old

Viennese clocks and furniture from the Biedermeier and Empire periods.

(Glasmuseum) Glass Museum C 3

1st District, Kärntner Strasse 26;
Tel. 5120508
Opening hours: Mon-Fri 9 am-5 pm, Sat 10 am-4 pm
On the upper floor of the glass speciality shop there is an exhibition of fine glass. Historic glass and the sample collection of Lobmeyr glass are on display.

(Globenmuseum) Museum of Globes C 3

1st District, Josefsplatz 1, 3rd floor;
Tel. 53410-297
Opening hours: Mon-Wed, Fri 11 am-noon, Thurs 2-3 pm
Valuable globes of the collection's 150 exhibits are the terrestial globe by Rainer Gemma Frisius (1535), two globes by Gerard Mercator and the terrestial globe by Peter Anich (1759).

(Glockenmuseum) Bell Museum

10th District, Senefeldergasse 70;
Tel. 6043460.
Reopening in 2004.
Records of how bells were manufactured in the former bell-foundry as well as a collection of famous church bells.

(Gold- und Silberschmiedemuseum) Gold and Silversmith Museum

7st District, Zieglergasse 22;
Tel. 5233388 + 5234096.
Opening hours: Wed 3-6 pm and by prior arrangement

(Haus der Musik) House of Music D 3

1st District, Seilerstätte 30;
Tel. 5164851

House of Music

Opening hours: daily 10 am-10 pm
The House of Music is located in the historic Palais Erzherzog Karl. In seven areas it makes music audible, visible and feelable. Visitors are encouraged to interactively play with music, are given historic information about music and experience unexpected sounds. Upstairs is the Museum of the Vienna Philharmonic Orchestra, in the apartment where their founder, composer and conductor Otto Nicolai, lived. The world-famous orchestra now presents itself where it was first born more than 150 years ago.

(Haus des Meeres) House of the Sea – Aquarium A 5

6th District, Esterházypark;
Tel. 5871417
Opening hours: daily 9 am-6 pm
The three-storey vivarium, created within the 2.5-m-thick concrete walls of the former anti-aircraft tower, was the first Austrian aquarium for ocean fish.

(Haydn-Museum mit Brahms-Gedenkraum) Haydn Museum with Brahms Memorial Room

6th District, Haydngasse 19;
Tel. 5961307
Opening hours: Tue-Sun 9 am-12:15 pm and 1-4:30 pm

The house where the composer Joseph Haydn (1732-1809) lived and died was converted into a museum in 1899. An exhibition in a small room documents the last years of Johannes Brahms' life (1833-1897), which were spent in Vienna.

(Heeresgeschichtliches Museum) Museum of Military History

3rd District, Arsenal, Objekt 18;
Tel. 79561-0
Opening hours: daily, except Friday, 9 am-5 pm
Byzantine architecture served as a model for this museum, constructed by Ludwig Förster and Theophil van Hansen on the grounds of the arsenal (1850-1857). The oldest planned museum in Vienna documents Austrian war history and the history of the imperial army from the Thirty Years' War to the First World War. Valuable weapons and uniforms are displayed and – in the navel museum – there is an impressive collection of model ships of the Imperial Navy.

Hofburg   B 3
(Rooms open to the public)
see Sights to See from A – Z

Hofburg

(Hofjagd- und Rüstkammer/ Sammlung alter Musik- instrumente) Collection of Arms and Armour and Collection of Historic Musical Instruments B 3

1st District, Neue Burg, Heldenplatz; Tel. 52524-0
Opening hours: daily, except Tue, 10 am-6 pm

Chair from the Apartments of Empress Maria Ludovica, c. 1810

(Kaiserliches Hofmobiliendepot) Court Furniture and Furnishings Depot

7th District, Mariahilfer Strasse 88; Tel. 5243357-0
Opening hours: daily, except Mon, 9 am-6 pm; Children's tours, Sun and Fri, 2:30 pm
This exhibition shows furnishings from the days of the Habsburgs and reveals details of imperial life. The exhibition also documents Viennese furniture art: from craftsmen who worked by appointment to the emperor to artists of the early 20th century.

(Kaiser-Franz-Joseph-Hut- museum und k. + k. Wein- schatzkammer) Emperor Franz Joseph Hat Museum and Imperial and Royal Wine Cellar

8th District, Piaristengasse 45/Restaurant Piaristenkeller; Tel. 4060193
Opening hours: daily, 6 pm-midnight, by prior telephone arrangement.

(Islamisches Zentrum) Islamic Centre

21st District, Hubertusdamm 17; Tel. 2630922
Opening hours: daily, except Fri, 9 am-5 pm. Guided group tours, Mon-Thurs, 9 am-noon, by prior arrangement

Josephinum A 1

9th District, Währingerstrasse 25/1; Tel. 4277-63401
Opening hours: Mon-Fri 9 am-3 pm, except holidays
In the Museum of the Institute of Medical History there are fascinating unique human wax figures that Joseph II commissioned to be made in Florence in the 18th century.

(Jüdisches Museum) Jewish Museum of the City of Vienna C 3

1st District, Dorotheergasse 11, Eskeles Palace; Tel. 5350431
Opening hours: daily, except Sat, 10 am-6 pm, Thurs 10 am-8 pm
The Baroque palace (18th century) houses this museum, refounded in 1993. Apart from the valuable collections (including Jewish ceremonial objects) there is a library. Adjacent to the museum is a bookshop and cafeteria.

(Kunstforum Wien) Art Forum, Vienna B 2

1st District, Freyung 8; Tel. 53733

Opening hours: daily 10 am-7 pm, Fri 10 am-9 pm (only during exhibitions) Since 1989 Austria's largest exhibition hall. Main focus of the programme that changes every year is "Classical Modern".

KunstHaus Wien

3rd District, Untere Weissgerberstrasse 13; Tel. 7120491
Opening hours: daily 10 am-7 pm. Guided tours Sun and holidays 11 am, noon and by prior arrangement, Tel. 712049512

KunstHaus Wien

The buildings Friedensreich Hundertwasser created (apart from the Hundertwasser House in Löwengasse and the Spittelauer Fernheizwerk) are a permanent exhibition of his work. International touring exhibitions can also be seen here.

⭐ (Kunsthistorisches Museum) Museum of Fine Art   B 4

Main building (Picture Gallery, Egyptian and Near Eastern Collection, Antiquities, Collection of Arts, Numismatic Collection)
1st District, Maria-Theresien-Platz; Tel. 52524-0
Opening hours: Tue-Sun 10 am-6 pm, Thurs till 9 pm

The museum is a legacy of the private collections belonging to the House of Habsburg and is one of the most famous art museums in the world. The core of the 10 sections (some are located outside the main building) is the **Picture Gallery** on the first floor. The most significant paintings are: the collection of old Dutch and Flemish paintings from the 15th and 16th centuries (Jan van Eyck, Bartholomäus Bruyn, Rogier van der Weyden; Hieronymus Bosch, Jan van Scorel), the greatest complete collection of works by the Flemish master Pieter Brueghel the Elder (the largest in the world); German painters of the 16th century (8 pictures by Albrecht Dürer, also Hans Holbein the Elder, Lucas Cranach the Elder, Albrecht Altdorfer); paintings by Peter Paul Rubens, Rembrandt van Rijn, Vermeer van Delft. In the West Wing are the works of Italian masters (Raffael Santi, Giorgione, Tizian, Veronese, Tintoretto, Canaletto), Spanish (Diego Velázquez) and several French masters.

The **Egyptian and Near Eastern Collection** on the mezzanine (Hochparterre) is one of the richest in the world: In addition to Egyptian mummies, sarcophagi and burial objects, the tomb of Prince Kaninisut (2,400 BC, Ancient Empire) is quite impressive.

In the **Antiquities** Greek, Etruscan and Roman works of art are united. The rich **Collection of Sculpture and Decorative Arts** reaches from the end of the 14th to the beginning of the 19th century, whereby the exhibits from the Renaissance predominate.

Leopold Museum (MQ)   AB 4

7th, District, Museumsplatz 1; Tel. 52570-0
Opening hours: daily, except Tue, 10

Egon Schiele, self-portrait

am-7 pm; Fri 10 am-9 pm; holidays, 10 am-7 pm

The Leopold Museum in Vienna's MuseumsQuartier, houses the world-famous, formerly private collection of Rudolf Leopold. Works from the 19th and 20th century Austrian school of painting are displayed on five exhibition levels in a pale limestone cube flooded with light. Of particular interest are excellent works produced in Vienna around the year 1900 by Gustav Klimt, Richard Gerstl, Koloman Moser and Oskar Kokoschka, as well as the world-wide most important Egon Schiele collection. Experience a picture of Austria at the Leopold Museum that is unique in its quality and density! Moreover, the museum shop offers a wide range of gift items. You can best enjoy a typical Viennese coffee at the Café Leopold, with its view of the main courtyard of the new MuseumsQuartier.

(Mozart Gedenkstätte im Figarohaus) Mozart Memorial Rooms in the Figaro House   D 3

1st District, Domgasse 5;
Tel. 5136294

Opening hours: daily, except Mon, 9 am-6 pm

Wolfgang Amadeus Mozart lived in the Figaro House from 1784 to 1787 and it was here that he composed "The Marriage of Figaro".

(Österr. Museum für angewandte Kunst) Austrian Museum of the Applied Arts   E 3

1st District, Stubenring 5;
Tel. 71136-0
Opening hours: Tue 10 am-midnight, Wed-Sun 10 am-6 pm
Here, in one of the oldest arts and crafts museums (founded in 1864), you can find exhibits from the Romantic Age up to the present. Special emphasis has been placed on the works of the "Wiener Werkstätte" (Jugendstil = Austrian art nouveau).

(Museum für Völkerkunde) Ethnographic Museum   B 3

1st District, Neue Burg, Heldenplatz;
Tel. 53430
Opening hours: daily, except Tue, 10 am-6 pm
The museum contains one of the largest ethnographic collections in the world. Of particular interest are Oceania with the James Cook Collection, West Africa and Ancient Mexico.

(Österr. Museum für Volkskunde) Austrian Folklore Museum

8th District, Laudongasse 15-19;
Tel. 4068905
Opening hours: daily, except Mon, 10 am-5 pm
In the former Garden Palace Schön-

brunn – designed by Lukas von Hildebrandt in 1706 – you can see models of settlements, houses and farms. Farmhouse interiors with original furniture are also on display. One can gain an insight into farmwork, crafts, folk music, folk dance and folk art.

(Museum Judenplatz Wien)
Museum Judenplatz Vienna   C 2

1st District, Judenplatz 8;
Tel. 5350431
Opening hours: Sun-Thurs, 10 am-6 pm; Fri 10 am-2 pm

Memorial on Judenplatz

MuseumsQuartier MQ
Vienna   AB 4

7th District, Museumsplatz 1;
Tel. 5235881
The passageways and walkways of the MuseumsQuartier Vienna are open 24 hours a day. The MQ Info & Ticket Centre is open daily from 10 am to 7 pm.
Opening hours:
Architecture Centre Vienna: daily 10 am-7 pm, Wed 10 am-9 pm;
Tel. 5223115
Art Cult Center/Tobacco Museum: Tue, Wed, Fri 10 am-5 pm, Thurs 10 am-7 pm, Sat, Sun, holidays 10 am-2 pm; Tel. 5261716
KUNSTHALLE vienna: Fri-Wed 10 am-7 pm, Thurs 10 am-10 pm;
Tel. 52189-14
Leopold Museum: see there.
MUMOK (Museum of Modern Art Ludwig Foundation Vienna): Tue-Sun

10 am-6 pm, Thurs 10 am-9 pm;
Tel. 52500
ZOOM Children's Museum: Mon-Fri 8:30 am-5 pm, Sat, Sun, holidays, school vacations 10 am-5:30 pm;
Tel. 5247908
One-of-a-kind scene for contemporary art and culture on 60,000 m².

Robert-Musil-Gedenkstätte
Memorial

3rd District, Rasumofskygasse 20;
Tel. 7131019
Opening hours: daily 10 am-1 pm

(Österr. Nationalbibliothek)
Austrian National Library   B 3

1st District, Josefsplatz 1;
Tel. 53410-0
Opening hours: Jan-Apr and Nov, Dec daily 10 am-2 pm, May-Oct daily 10 am-4 pm, Thurs 10 a-7 pm
The Baroque building, joined to the Hofburg, contains about 2.5 million books, 200,000 of which are in the Great Hall (Prunksaal) alone including the 15,000 gold-decorated volumes from Prince Eugene's library. Other special exhibits are the collecions of printed works and the manuscript, incunabulum, globe, map, papyrus and portrait collections, the picture library, the music and theatre collections.

Great Hall of the Austrian National Library

(Naturhistorisches Museum) Museum of Natural History B 3

1st District, Maria-Theresien-Platz; Tel. 52177-0
Opening hours: daily, except Tue, 9 am-6:30 pm, Wed 9 am-9 pm.
Rooftop tour: Mon 5, 6:30 pm, groups by prior arrangement.
The foundation for the museum was a collection of natural history objects belonging to Emperor Franz I. In 1889 the twin-construction was built and it now houses the Museum of Natural History. Departments: Minerology/Petrography with the world-famous Meteorite Collection and the Gemstone Room (117-kg topaz, "Bouquet of Jewels"); Geology/Paleontology with fossils, skeletons of Ice Age mammals such as cave-bears; the Prehistoric Collection – survey of the cultural development, especially in the Danube and Alpine regions (Venus of Willendorf, findings from Hallstatt in Upper Austria during the Iron Age – the "Hallstatt Age"); Anthropology, Botany (4 million objects) and Zoology (830 vertebrates and fish, 3 million beetles, 3 million butterflies and 4 million other insects). There is a special Children's Room.

(Pathologisch-Anatomisches Bundesmuseum) Federal Museum of Pathological Anatomy

9th District, Spitalgasse 2, 13. Hof "Narrenturm"; Tel. 4068672
Opening hours: Wed 3-6 pm, Thurs 8-11 am, 1st Sat of every month, 10 am-1 pm; closed holidays.

Phonomuseum

6th District, Mollardgasse 8; Tel. 5811159
Opening hours: Wed 6-8 pm

Planetarium

2nd District, Oswald-Thomas-Platz 1 (at the Riesenrad); Tel. 7295494-0

Guided tours by telephone appointment.

Prater Museum

2nd District, Oswald-Thomas-Platz 1; Tel. 7267683
Opening hours: Tue-Fri 9 am-12:15 pm and 1-4:30 pm, Sat, Sun and holidays 2-6:30 pm

(Puppen- und Spielzeugmuseum) Doll and Toy Museum C 2

1st District, Schulhof 4, 1st floor; Tel. 5356860
Opening hours: Tue-Sun and holidays 10 am-6 pm

(Rauchfangkehrermuseum) Chimney-Sweep Museum

4th District, Klagbaumgasse 4/2; Tel. 51450-2275
Opening hours: Sun 10-noon

(Sammlung religiöser Volkskunst) Collection of Religious Folk Art C 3

with Old Monastery Apothecary (Klosterapotheke)
1st District, Johannesgasse 8; Tel. 5121337
Opening hours: Wed 10 am-5 pm

★ (Schatzkammer) Secular and Ecclesiastical Treasuries B 3

1st District, Hofburg, Schweizerhof; Tel. 52524-0
Opening hours: daily, except Tue, 10 am-6 pm
Secular and sacred treasures, jew-

ellery and memorabilia of inestimable value from the Habsburg dynasty are on display. Showpieces of the Secular Treasury include the imperial jewels of the Holy Roman Empire from the 10th and 11th centuries – the emperor's crown, the imperial orb, sceptre and sword, imperial crucifix and book of the gospels (Carolingian crimson codex, end of 8th century) – and the so-called Burgundian Treasure with the insignia of the Order of the Golden Fleece.

Arnold-**Schönberg Center**

3rd District, Zaunergasse 1-3;
Tel. 7121888
Opening hours: Mon-Fri, except holidays, 10 am-5 pm

(**Schokolademuseum**)
Chocolate Museum

23rd District, Willendorfer Gasse 2-8;
Tel. 6672110-0
Opening hours: Mon-Fri 10 am-4 pm

Schubert Gedenkstätten
Memorials/Schubert Museum
(the composer's birthplace) with
Adalbert-Stifter-Memorial-
Rooms

9th District, Nussdorfer Strasse 54;
Tel. 3173601
Opening hours: daily, except Mon,
9 am-12:15 pm and 1-4:30 pm
This is where Franz Schubert was born in 1797.
The room where Schubert died
4th District, Kettenbrückengasse 6;
Tel. 5816730
Opening hours: daily, except Mon,
1-4:30 pm

Secession   B 4

1st District, Friedrichstrasse 12;
Tel. 5875307
Opening hours: Tue-Sun and holidays 10 am-6 pm, Thurs 10 am-8 pm
The Jugendstil building's character-

istic feature is the filigree gilded sparkling globe, representing a stylized laurel tree (dubbed by the Viennese the "golden cabbage head"). Joseph Olbrich, a pupil of Otto Wagner, created the exhibition hall for the group of Secessionist artists under Gustav Klimt in 1898. The "Beethoven Frieze" (its theme is the composer's 9th symphony) by Gustav Klimt can be seen here. The frieze had to be repurchased by the Austrian state and restored. There are also temporary exhibitions on contemporary art in the building.

(Wiener **Strassenbahnmuseum**)
Vienna **Tram Museum**

3rd District, Ludwig-Koeßler-Platz;
Tel. 7909-44900
Opening hours: May-Oct, Sat, Sun,
holidays 9-4 pm

Johann-**Strauss-Wohnung/**
Apartment

2nd District, Praterstrasse 54
(Donauwalzerhaus); Tel. 2140121
Opening hours: Tue-Sun 9 am-12:15
pm and 1-4:30 pm
Johann Strauss the Younger, the composer of the "Blue Danube" waltz lived here from 1863 to 1870.

(**Synagoge**) Synagogue   D 2

1st District, Seitenstettengasse 2;
Tel. 5350431
Guided tours daily, except Sat and holidays, 11:30 am and 3 pm

(**Technisches Museum**)
Technical Museum

14th District, Mariahilfer Strasse 212;
Tel. 89998-6000
Opening hours: Mon-Wed, Fri, Sat 9 am-6 pm, Thurs 9 am-8 pm, Sun and holidays 10 am-6 pm
The museum, founded in 1908, shows the development of technology from the earliest days right up to the present. Among the 80,000 ex-

hibits emphasis is laid on Austrian inventions: the first Kaplan turbine in the world, the Marcus four-cycle gasoline engine (1887), a model of gas installation for street lights (1818) at the "Kärntertor" (former city gate), Thonet's bentwood furniture from 1849, Ressel's marine screw propeller, the sewing machine invented by Madersperger (1814). The various workshops are of particular interest, as well as a collection of bicycles, old model aeroplanes and the Lilienthal glider, high above the floor of the main hall.

(Österr. **Theatermuseum**) Austrian **Theatre Museum**   C 3

1st District, Lobkowitzplatz 2; Tel. 5128800-0
Opening hours: Tue-Sun 10 am-5 pm, Wed 10 am-8 pm, guided tours by prior arrangement
1st District, Hanuschgasse 3; Tel. 5122427
Opening hours: Tue-Fri 10 am-noon, 1-4 pm, Sat, Sun and holidays 1-4 pm
Rooms commemorating various famous actors.

(Uhrenmuseum der Stadt Wien) Clock Museum of the City of Vienna   C 2

1st District, Schulhof 2; Tel. 5332265
Opening hours: Tue-Sun 9 am-4:30 pm
The three floors of the 300-year-old Obizzi Palace are replete with clocks and watches from all periods.

UNO City

22nd District, Wagramer Strasse 3-5; Tel. 26060-3328
Guided tours Mon-Fri 11 am and 2 pm; groups by prior arrangement.

(Urania-Sternwarte) Urania Observatory   E 2

1st District, Uraniastrasse 1;

Tel. 7295494-0
Reopening in 2004.

(Virgilkapelle) St. Virgil's Chapel/Collection of Historic Ceramics   C 3

1st District, Stephansplatz; Tel. 5135842
Opening hours: Tue-Sun 1-4:30 pm

Otto-**Wagner-Wohnung/ Apartment**

7th District, Döblergasse 4; Tel. 5232233
Opening hours: only on request

(Wien Museum Karlsplatz) Vienna Museum Karlsplatz   C 4/5

4th District, Karlsplatz; Tel. 5058747-84021
Opening hours: Tue-Sun 9 am-6 pm
The exhibits, displayed in two storeys, give us an insight into Vienna's rich history and into the art and culture of the city. The museum's collection spans seven milleniums. Beginning with finds from the Early Stone Age, it includes the Roman Vindobona, medieval Vienna, the period of Turkish Sieges, the blossoming of the city during the Baroque Era, the Congress of Vienna, Biedermeier Vienna and the revolutionary year 1848 up to the "Gründerzeit", the Ringstrasse Era and with the Viennese Jugendstil (Adolf Loos Lounge, paintings by Klimt and Schiele) the 20th century.

(Wiener Kriminalmuseum) Vienna Criminal Museum

2nd District, Grosse Sperlgasse 24; Tel. 2144678
Opening hours: Tue-Sun 10 am-5 pm

(Wiener Ziegelmuseum) Vienna Brick Museum

14th District, Penzinger Strasse 59; Tel. 8972852
Opening hours: every first and third Sun in the month 10-noon

A visit to the ★ **Prater** is always fun: The "Wurstelprater" with its amusement park and the **Giant Ferris Wheel (Riesenrad)** is always enticing. Perhaps you would like to take a lift on the miniature train (Liliputbahn) – it goes from the Volksprater to Stadionallee and back – or how about a quick Wild West game at the adventure playground with its Wild West fort and waterfall on the Jesuit meadow (Jesuitenwiese)! Perhaps you can manage both – and then a visit to the

Planetarium
2nd District, Prater, Oswald-Thomas-Platz 1; Tel. 7295494
Guided tours: by telephone reservation
The **Urania Observatory** is quite an experience for little astronomers.
1st District, Uraniastrasse 1;
Tel. 7295494
Reopening in 2004.

Children all love animals:
In ★ **Schönbrunn Zoo,** the oldest zoo on earth, animals from all over the world can be admired. There is also a Petting Zoo and a playground. 13th District, Schönbrunner Schlosspark (Hietzinger Tor); Tel. 8779294-0
Zoo: Opening hours: daily! Jan, Nov and Dec 9 am-4:30 pm, Feb 9 am-5 pm, March and Oct 9 am-5:30 pm, April 9 am-6 pm, May to Sept 9 am-6:30 pm;
Tel. 8779294-0
Zoo favourites include elephants, koalas, polar bears, pandas, giraffes etc. And don't forget a visit to the tropical jungle house, the aquariums and terrariums.
The nighttime tours of the zoo have become a major attraction. These tours at dusk using low-level light reinforcement are a good way to see the animals' nocturnal behavior. Telephone reservations for these tours are a must.
Worth a visit in **Schönbrunn Park** are **the Palm and Desert House** and the **Maze**.
Irrgarten (Maze): Opening hours: Apr-June and Sept daily 9 am-6 pm, July and Aug daily 9 am-7 pm;

Giant panda in Schönbrunn Zoo

Oct daily 9 am-5 pm, Nov 10 am-4 pm; Tel. 81113-239

Palmenhaus (Palm House): Opening hours: May-Sept daily 9:30 am-5:30 pm; Oct-Apr 9:30 am-4:30 pm; Tel. 8775087-406

Wüstenhaus (Desert House): Opening hours: May-Sept 9-6 pm, Oct-Apr 9-5 pm; Tel. 877508

Schmetterlingshaus (Butterfly House), Hofburg/Burggarten: Opening hours: April to Oct Mon-Fri 10 am-4:45 pm, Sat, Sun and holidays 10 am-6:15 pm, Nov to March daily 10 am-3:45 pm; Tel. 5338570
You can take photographs of brightly coloured exotic butterflies in amongst tropical plants.

In the **House of the Sea – Aquarium (Haus des Meeres)** the fish and sea creatures are fed at 3 pm every day.
6th District, Esterházypark; Tel. 5871417
Opening hours: daily 9 am-6 pm

Museums with guided tours for children
In the **Museum of Natural History (Naturhistorisches Museum)** you can see a dinosaur's skeleton. In the Children's Room you can stroke the animals and touch the stones in the mineral collection.
1st District, Maria-Theresien-Platz; Tel. 52177-0
Opening hours: daily, except Tue, 9 am-6:30 pm, Wed 9 am-9 pm

1st District, Maria-Theresien-Platz; Tel. 52524-0
Opening hours: daily, except Mon, 10 am-6 pm, Thurs 10 am-9 pm

Doll and Toy Museum (Puppen- und Spielzeugmuseum)
1st District, Schulhof 4/I; Tel. 5356860
Opening hours: Tue-Sun and holidays 10 am-6 pm

Circus and Clown Museum
2nd District, Karmelitergasse 9; Tel. 21106-02127
Opening hours: Wed 5:30-7 pm, Sat 2:30-5 pm, Sun 10am-noon

Theatre
Heuschreck, 7th District, Kaiserstrasse 33, Tel. 5239180
Marionettentheater (Schloss Schönbrunn/Hofratstrakt), 13 District, Tel. 8173247
Metropolino, 17th District, Hernalser Hauptstrasse 55, Tel. 4077740-7
Moki Mobiles Kindertheater, 4th District, Blechturmgasse 14, Tel. 5059806

Vienna Holiday Games
Children can play games and make things, go on excursions and see exhibitions in July and August, in the Christmas holidays and in the mid-term break in February. Information as to events and leisure-time activities for children can be obtained from the wien Xtra Jugendinfo, 1st District, Babenbergerstrasse 1; Tel. 1799 (Mon-Fri noon-7 pm, Sat 10 am-7 pm). Internet surfing for young people.

Children's Outdoor Swimming Pools

An exceptional feature in the extensive variety of swimming pools in Vienna: admission only for children between the ages of 6 and 15, admission is free of charge. For more information: pool telephone 60112 (Mon-Fri 10 am-6 pm).

Playgrounds in the woods

Besides the playgrounds in the parks of the Inner City, Vienna has laid out a great many playgrounds in its recreation areas.

2nd District
Prater: Jesuitenwiese (tram line N; Bus Line 4A, 80A Wittelsbachstrasse); Rosenwasser near Heustadelwasser: 2 playgrounds (bus lines 77A, 80B)

10th District
Laaer Wald: Böhmischer Prater, Unterwald, Löwygrube, Festwiese (all bus lines 68A Urselbrunnengasse); Vogental, Eisenbahnersportplatz (for both: Bus line 68A Theodor-Sickel-Gasse)
Wienerberg (tram line 67 Wienerfeldgasse)

11th District
Neugebäude (bus line 73A Hörtengasse); Meidlgasse (bus line 72A, 73A Kaiserebersdorfer Friedhof)

13th District
Lainzer Tiergarten (Zoo, Tel. 8041315. Opening hours: from mid-Feb to mid-Nov from 8 am till dusk):

Hermes Villa in Lainzer Zoo

Lainzer Tor, Hermesvilla, Hirschgstemm, Rohrhaus (all bus lines 60B Lainzer Tor); Gütenbachtor (bus line 153 Gütenbachstrasse); Hackenbergwiese (S45, S50, U4, bus line 53B Hütteldorf)

14th District
Dehnepark (tram line 49 Hütteldorfer Strasse/Rosentalgasse); Recreational area Steinhofgründe (bus line 46B/146B Feuerwache "Am Steinhof")

16th District
Savoyenstrasse (bus line 46B/146B Schloss Wilhelminenberg); Steinbruchwiese (bus line 46B/146B)

17th District
Schwarzenbergpark, former Rohrerbad-Gelände (both bus line 43B Marswiese)

18th District
Michaelerwald (bus line 43B Artariastrasse)

19th District
Gspöttgraben (bus line 39A terminus Sievering); Cobenzl (bus line 38A), Josefinenhütte (bus line 38A); Krapfenwaldgasse (bus line 38A); Hermannskogel, Jägerwiese (both bus line 38A Sulzwiese or Cobenzl)

21st District
Falkenberg, Magdalenhof (for both bus line 32A Anton-Böck-Gasse); Schwarzlackenau, Christian-Bucher-Gasse (bus line 33B Überfuhrstrasse)

22nd District
Grünverbindung Thonetgasse (bus line 25A, 31A Eipeldauer Strasse/Jüptnergasse)

23rd District
Pappelteich (bus lines 60A, 153 Kalksburg); Gasthaus (restaurant) Schiessstätte (bus line 60A Maurer-Lange-Gasse/Kasernengasse)
Bisamberg, Lower Austria: Gamshöhe, Elisabethhöhe (both S3 Langenzersdorf, bus line 32A Strebersdorfer Platz)

The Spanish Riding School

The oldest riding school in the world was founded in 1572 by Emperor Maximilian II. Up till the present day Baroque horsemanship, the high art of equestrianism, has been kept up. The noble dressage horses, the Lipizzaner, are descendants of the Spanish breed of horse used in the 16th century, a cross of Spanish and Arab horses. The imperial stud farm was in Lipizza, in today's Slovenia, and was the home of the white horses for over 300 years. In 1918, after the fall of the monarchy when the borders shifted, the riding school's stud farm had to be moved. The state stud farm has been in Piber in western Styria since 1920.

The dark brown to grey foals take four to ten years to turn pure white. When they are three and a half years old, training for performances in the Spanish Riding School begins for the stallions. The horses learn to bring difficult but natural movements to the highest perfection. Originally the high art of equestrianism was applied on the battlefield and served to protect the rider. At the performances the "Airs on the Ground" (piaffe, passage, pirouette) and the "Airs Above the Ground" (levade, courbette, capriole) are demonstrated; riding groups also perform the pas de trois (a threesome dance), the polonaise or the quadrille. The performances take place in Baroque surroundings in the Winter Riding School, built by Joseph Emanuel Fischer von Erlach in 1735. The Lipizzaners' stables lie opposite in the Renaissance building of the Stallburg. The veteran stallions return to Piber, where they procreate and usually reach a ripe old age.

**Spanish Riding School
(Spanische Hofreitschule)**
1st District, Josefsplatz
Information on performances under tel. 5339031

POPULAR EXCURSIONS

Vienna, a city with over a million inhabitants, can deem itself lucky: not only are there plenty of parks and green areas in the Inner City, but the green belt surrounding the outer districts – the Wienerwald (Vienna Woods) and the protected Danube meadowlands – offer numerous trails for relaxing walks, among which are the following.

HIKES IN VIENNA

1 From Nussdorf (terminus for tram line D) through the vineyards high above the River Danube, with a wonderful view of the city, ★ **Kahlenberg,** 484 m. Back via the Josefinenhütte and Kahlenbergerdorf (Kahlenberg village). This hike takes approx. 4 hours (11 km).

2 From Sievering (terminus for bus line 39A) via Salmannsdorfer Höhe up to **Hermannskogel,** 542 m, the highest point in Vienna. Back via Cobenzl. This hike takes 3-4 hours (10 km).

3 From Dornbach (terminus for the bus line 43B, tram line 43) via Neuwaldegg and Schwarzenbergpark up to **Hameau;** back via Dreimarkstein and Michaelerwald (Michaeler Forest). This hike takes 3-4 hours.

From the trail no. 4 over Wilhelminenberg you can get a good view of the dome of the Church "am Steinhof" on Baumgartner Höhe. Otto Wagner planned the church (1904-1907), which is pure Jugendstil, and Koloman Moser designed the stained-glass windows.

Stained-glass window by Koloman Moser

Kartengrundlage: © Mairs Geographischer Verlag, Ostfildern

④ From Hütteldorf/Rosentalgasse (tram line 49) through Dehnepark to **Jubiläumswarte.** Back via Wilhelminenberg. This hike takes approx. 3 hours (7.2 km).

⑤ From Stammersdorf (terminus of the tram line 31, bus 125) among vineyards up to **Bisamberg** where more meadows invite you to play and rest. Via the wood Herrenholz back to Stammersdorf – in the "Kellergassen" (lanes bordered by wine cellars) and a well-deserved snack. This hike takes 3-4 hours (10.3 km).

⑥ From Rodaun (terminus tram line 60, bus 60A) over the wooded crest of Zugberg to **Wiener Hütte.** Via the Valley of the Reichen Liesing to **Maurer Forest,** back over Antonshöhe and Georgenberg. This hike takes approx. 4 hours.

⑦ From Reumannplatz (terminus of the U1, tram line 6) on the southern outskirts of the city through Laaer Forest and Böhmischer Prater to the recreation park **Laaer Berg.**

⑧ The hike over the plateau of Sophienalpe with its extensive beech woods is one of the most typical Vienna Woods trails. From Vorderhainbach on the western outskirts of Vienna (bus stop Gasthaus/restaurant "Grüner Jäger", bus line 449) via Mostalm to **Sophienalpe,** on to Rieglerhütte, through Halterbach Valley, back past Laudon-Grab. This hike takes 3-4 hours.

⑨ From Praterstern through Volksprater to the area called **Grüner Prater** (Green Prater) in the peaceful meadowland between the River Danube and the Danube Canal, now a nature reserve, and back again. This hike takes 3-4 hours.

⑩ The great **circular tour round Vienna** (120 km) – divided into 6 stages – goes from "Donauinsel" (Danube Island) (U1 station) up to Kahlenberg, then on to Weidlingau and from there to Liesing, on the southern outskirts of the city to Freudenau, then to the outer districts beyond the Danube to Gerasdorf. From the northern outskirts of Vienna back again to the Danube Island.
Each stage of this hike takes 3-6 hours.

Always a good idea: a walk through the Vienna Woods

Lainzer Zoo

From Lainzer Tor (terminus bus line 60B) to the Hermesvilla, on to Rohrhaus and **Kaltbründlberg**, 508 m, via Gasthaus (restaurant) Hirschgstemm, back to Linzer Tor. This hike takes 3½ hours.

Zoo: Opening hours: from mid-Feb to mid-Nov from 8 am till dusk. Tel. 8041315.

Emperor Fanz Joseph had the Hermesvilla built for his spouse Sisi as a hunting lodge (1882/86 by Karl von Hasenauer). Today there are temporary exhibitions from the Vienna Museum Karslplatz in the rooms designed by Victor Tilgner and Hans Makart.

Opening hours: Apr-Sept: Tue-Sun and holidays 10 am-6 pm; Oct-Mar: Tue-Sun and holidays 9 am-4:30 pm. Tel. 804132

Kaisermühlen on the Danube

Upper Lobau

From Grossenzersdorf (terminus bus line 26A) over the Kasern Bridge through the legally protected meadowland to the Lobau Museum (with many nature exhibits from the primeval landscape which is rich in wildlife and notable for its botany) on via Napoleonstein, Esslinger Furt, Stadlerfurt and back to Grossenzersdorf. This hike takes 2½ hours (also recommendable as a biking tour).

Danube Island

On foot or by bike from Langenzersdorf (railway station) across the bridge to the New Danube Island (parallel cycle tracks and footpaths). Across the New Danube you can see over to the Danube Tower and UNO-City. This hike takes 6 hours (30 km); an interruption is possible. The last bridge, the Wehr 2-Bridge, leads you over to the oil harbour, on the S-Bahn (suburban railway) Station Lobau or to bus stops.

Schönbrunn Palace Park

A walk from Hietzing (underground station) to the Palace Park. Along the avenue bordered by trees, trimmed in a wall-like fashion up to the Gloriette: beautiful view of Vienna. On to the Tyrolean Garden, past the Palm and Desert House and then to the zoo. This hike (not including tours) takes 2 hours.

Nature trails

Laaer Forest (10th District)
Neugebäude (11th District)
Lainzer Zoo (13th District)
Dehnepark (14th District)
Wilhelminenberg (16th District)
Schafberg (18th District)
Bisamberg (21st District)
Lobau (22nd District)
Danube park – nature trail – protection of birds (22nd District)
Maurer Forest (23rd District)
Nature Trail Purkersdorf

EXCURSIONS IN THE SURROUNDING AREA

Baden – Gumpoldskirchen

The spa of Baden, 20 km south of Vienna, has been especially popular with the Viennese since the beginning of the 19th century. A number of artists have come to live here, and Emperor Franz I spent the summer months in Baden between 1803 and 1834.

A visit can also be combined with a hike in the famous wine-growing village of Gumpoldskirchen along Beethoven Trail No. 40. You can go back along the Erste Wiener Hochquellenleitung (aqueduct). This hike takes 4½ hours.

Heiligenkreuz

The Cistercian monastery, founded in the 12th century, dominates Heiligenkreuz in the southern Vienna Woods (34 km from Vienna). The Romanesque abbey is well worth a visit with its valuable stained-glass windows (around 1300), richly carved Baroque choir stalls by Giovanni Giuliani (1707) as well as altar pictures by Martino Altomonte. Thirteen Babenbergs are interred in the Gothic chapter hall. There are more objects worth seeing in the abbey museum.

Nearby lies the former hunting lodge **Mayerling** (now a convent) where, in 1889, Crown Prince Rudolf and Baroness Mary Vetsera tragically committed suicide.

Baden bei Wien, Main Square

Augustinian Abbey in Klosterneuburg

Klosterneuburg

This town, surrounded by vine-yards, lies 12 km north of Vienna on the River Danube. The former seat of the Babenbergs is famous for its Augustinian Abbey, one of the largest Austrian wine produc-ers. the "Verdun Altar" in the abbey church and the Baroque abbey and abbey museum are worth visiting. (A Babenberg family tree and the early Gothic "Klosterneuburg Madonna" can be seen here.) Aus-tria's largest abbey library (over 200,000 volumes) is only accessi-ble for those doing scientific re-search.

Marchfeld

In this fertile countryside east of Vi-enna, Austria's bread basket, you come across charming Baroque castles. In the former hunting grounds outside the gates of the residence many noblemen built their castles and hunting lodges (Castle Eckartsau, Niederweiden, Schlosshof, Marchegg).
A popular place for excursions to the north of the Marchfeld is Gänserndorf with its unique Safari Park, the only one in Austria. In the extensive park you can see ele-phants, zebras and other animals roaming free.

Petronell-Carnuntum

About 42 km down the Danube ex-cavations from the once famous Roman town of Carnuntum, in the community of Petronell, can be viewed (open-air museum). The Museum Carnuntinum in the neigh-bouring Deutsch Altenburg pro-vides a closer look at the Roman culture of its provinces in the first four centuries AD.

Palace Park Laxenburg

A trip to Laxenburg to the south-east of Vienna is worthwhile (15 km). The court mainly spent the summers in the former imperial palace. A walk round the Palace Park with its centuries-old trees, an example of romantic landscape art, takes approx. 1¼ hours.

KOMPASS Map of Hikes 209 "Wiener-wald" (1:35 000) is recommendable for your hikes and excursions.

Important Tips – Information

Area code for Vienna: 01 – Postal codes: A-1010 to A-1230 Vienna

INFORMATION

Tourist Information
1st District, Albertinaplatz 1;
Tel. 24555
Opening hours: daily 9 am-7 pm

Vienna Tourist Office
Information and hotel reservations
Tel. 24555, Fax 24555-666
Opening hours: daily 9 am-7 pm
info@wien.info
www.wien.info
Mailing address: 1025 Vienna,
Austria

City Information in Vienna's City
Hall, 1st District, Friedrich-
Schmidt-Platz; Tel. 52550.
Opening hours: Mon-Fri 8 am-6
pm, Sun and holidays 8 am-4 pm

Vienna Xtra Jugendinfo
1st District, Babenbergerstrasse 1;
Tel. 1799 (Mon-Fri noon-7 pm, Sat
10 am-7 pm). Internet surfing for
young people.

Lower Austria Information
Only for telephone information and
to order brochures.
Tel. 53610-6200

Austrian Holiday Information
4th District, Margaretenstrasse 1;
Tel. 5872000, Fax 58866-48

Austrian Tourist Information Office
1st District, Friedrichstrasse 7;
Tel. 58800-510

For travel by train
Travel offices at Westbahnhof (railway station for trains going west)
(6:15 am-11 pm) and Südbahnhof
(railway station for trains going
south).
Opening hours: May-Oct 6:30-10
pm, Nov-April 6:30-9 pm

For travel by air
Tourist information in the arrivals
lounge at the Wien-Schwechat airport.
Opening hours: daily Oct-May 8:30
am-10 pm, June-Sept 8:30 am-11
pm

For travel by boat
Round trips and evening dancing
on board from May to Oct Information and bookings: DDSG Schiff-
fahrt GmbH, Blue Danube, 1st District, Friedrichstrasse 7;
Tel. 58880-0

The "Sacher," a Viennese institution

Information as to **hotels and guest-houses** in Vienna can be acquired at the Vienna Tourist Office – there is a summer and winter hotel list. The Lower Austrian Information Office is responsible for accommodations outside the city.

The "Mitwohnzentrale" can help you find **private accommodations** (short stays for at least 3 days): 8th District, Laudongasse 18; Tel. 4026061; Mon-Fri 10 am-6 pm

Youth Hostels

Turmherberge "Don Bosco", 3rd District, Lechnerstrasse 12; Tel. 7131494; open March-Nov

Jugendherberge Myrthengasse/ Neustiftgasse, 7th District, Myrthengasse 7; Tel. 5236316; Fax 5235849; open year-round

Kolping House Wien-Meidling, 12th District, Bendlgasse 10-12; Tel. 8135487, Fax 8122130; open year-round

Jugendgästehaus der Stadt Wien Hütteldorf-Hacking, 13th District, Schlossberggasse 8; Tel. 8770263, Fax 87702632; open year-round

Hostel Ruthensteiner, 15th District, Robert-Hamerling-Gasse 24; Tel. 8934202; open year-round

Schlossherberge am Wilhelminenberg, 16th District, Savoyenstrasse 2; Tel. 4858503-700, Fax 4858503-702; open year-round

Haus Döbling, 19th District, Gymnasiumstrasse 85; Tel. 3695490-0; open July-Sept

Jugendgästehaus Wien Brigittenau, 20th District, Friedrich-Engels-Platz 24; Tel. 3328294-0, Fax 3308379; open year-round

Jugendgästehaus, Hirschengasse 25, 6th District, Tel. 5977600

Information: Österreichisches Jugendherbergswerk (ÖJHW), 1st District, Helferstorfer Strasse 4; Tel. 5331833

Österreichischer Jugendherbergsverband, 1st District, Schottenring 28; Tel. 5335353

Niederöster. and Wiener Jugendherbergswerk, 7th District, Mariahilfer Strasse 24; Tel. 5237158

Camping Grounds

Stadt Wien West I, 14th District, Hüttelbergstrasse 40; Tel. 9142314, Fax 9113594; mid-July-August

Stadt Wien West II, 14th District, Hüttelbergstrasse 80; Tel. 9142314; Fax 9113594; open year-round (closed Feb)

Aktiv Camping "Neue Donau", 22nd District, Am Kleehäufl/Am Kaisermühlendamm 119; Tel. 2024010, Fax 2032823; mid-May to mid-Sept

Camping Rodaun, 23rd District, An der Au 2/Breitenfurterstrasse 487; Tel. = Fax 8884154; March-Nov

Camping Süd, 23rd District, Breitenfurterstrasse 296; Tel. 8673649, Fax 8675843

Klosterneuburg Donaupark-Camping, 3400 Klosterneuburg, In der Au 4, Austria; Tel. 02243/25877

Schloss Laxenburg, 2361 Laxenburg/Lower Austria, Austria Münchendorfer Strasse; Tel. 02236/71333, Fax 73966

GUIDED TOURS AND ROUND TRIPS

Tour Guide Agency
Travel Point, 9th District, Alserbach-strasse 11; Tel. 3194243
Vienna Guide Service, 9th District, Sommerhaidenweg 124;
Tel. 443094, Fax 4402825
Tour guides can be recognized by their official tour guide badge and ID.

City Walks
The Vienna tour guides offer over 50 walking tours (also in foreign languages) according to selected themes. You can travel through the city's epochs, gain insight into Vienna's sagas, legends and crime chronicles as well as become acquainted with underground Vienna or follow in the footsteps of Mozart, Beethoven, Schubert, Freud or the "Third Man" (original scenes of the film made from Graham Greene's novel on post World War II Vienna) – this tour takes approx. 2 hours, 3-25 persons possible per tour. Up-to-date programme and brochure available at Tourist-Information, 1st District, Albertinaplatz.

Sightseeing Tours (by bus)
If you wish to see as many sights of the city in as short a time as possible, this is the way to do it.
Vienna Sightseeing Tours, 4th District, Graf-Starhemberg-Gasse 25;
Tel. 7124683-0
Cityrama Sightseeing Travel Agency, 1st District, Börsegasse 1;
Tel. 53413-0
Rundfahrten "Modernes Wien" (Tours of Modern Vienna), City Hall Information; Tel. 4000-81050
Alternative Sightseeing Tour Stattwerkstatt, Verein zur Vermittlung des wirklichen Wien (an association wishing to reveal the "true" Vienna) 9th District, Kolingasse 6;
Tel. 3173384

Per Pedes, city and cultural tours, 5th District, Einsiedlergasse 6;
Tel. = Fax 5449668

Sightseeing Tours (by boat)
3-hour round trip (it is possible only to go on one stage of the round trip) from May-October, departure at the quay of the "Donau-Dampfschiff-fahrtsgesellschaft" (DDSG) Blue Danube, Schwedenplatz. Round trips and evening dancing on board from May-Oct Information and bookings: DDSG, 1st District, Friedrichstrasse 7; Tel. 58880-0

Oldtimer Tramway
A two-hour ride with a tram from the year 1929: from the Old City to Schönbrunn Palace and on to the Giant Ferris Wheel; board at Karlsplatz/Otto-Wagner-Pavillion; May to beginning of Oct, Wed and Sat 1:30 pm, Sun and holidays 10 am and 1:30 pm. Information and bookings: Tel. 8921334-0 and 7860303

Sightseeing Tours (by bike)
Sporty tourists can admire the architecture of Ringstrasse, the Viennese Jugendstil or the Viennese "jungle" in the Lobau on a biking tour. Information: Bike & Guide, 2nd District, Rueppgasse 2/9;
Tel. = Fax 2121135

Hackney Cabs
The traditional Viennese horse-drawn and cabs offer two tours: the Old City tour, approx. 20 minutes and the Old City and Ringstrasse tour takes about 30 minutes.
The carriages await you at Stephansplatz, Albertinaplatz and Heldenplatz.

City Tours by Air
Information, Flughafen (airport) Wien-Schwechat; Tel. 7007-0

Augarten Porcelain

TRAVELLING AND TRANSPORT

Travelling by Car
Automobile Associations
ARBÖ Regional Office, 15th District,
Mariahilfer Strasse 180;
Tel. 89121-0
ÖAMTC Regional Office,
1st District, Schubertring 1-3;
Tel. 71199
Breakdown services
ARBÖ   Tel. 123
ÖAMTC   Tel. 120

Car Rental
Arac: 23rd District,
Brunnerstrasse 85;
Tel. 86616-0, Fax 8698640

Avis: 1st District,
Opernring 5;
Tel. 5876241 und 5874900;
Flughafen (airport) Wien-Schwechat,
Tel. 7007-32700

Barnea: 6th District,
Esterházygasse 6;
Tel. 5862454

Buchbinder: 3rd District,
Schlachthausgasse 38;
Tel. 71750-0, Fax 71750-22

Europcar: 1st District,
Schubertring 9;
Tel. 7146717, Fax 7121279

Flott: 6th District,
Mollardgasse 44;
Tel. 5973402-0, Fax 5967429

Hartl: 5th District,
Margarethen Gürtel 41;
Tel. 5444343, Fax 5444343-9

Hertz: city office, 1st District,
Kärntner Ring 17,
Tel. 5128677, Fax 5125034

Further car rentals in the yellow
pages under "Autoverleih".

Travelling by Train
Westbahnhof: terminus station for
rail link to the west of Austria, Germany, Switzerland, Italy.

Südbahnhof: terminus station for rail
link to the south and east, the south
of Austria, Italy, Hungary, Slovenia,
Croatia.

Franz-Josefs-Bahnhof: terminus station for rail link to the north of Austria, Slovakia, the Czech Rebublic.

Bahnhof Wien-Mitte: S-Bahn regional rail link

Bahnhof Nord/Praterstern: local rail service

Schedule, price information, tickets and reservations, Tel. 05/1717 (local call charge inside Austria), daily 24 hours; www.oebb.at

ÖBB = Österreichische Bundesbahnen (Austrian Federal Railways), information, Tel. 93000

Travel offices at Franz-Josef-Bahnhof, Tel. 93000-31020

Travel offices at Bahnhof Wien Mitte, Tel. 93000-31070

Travel offices at Südbahnhof, Tel. 93000-31050

Travel offices at Westbahnhof, Tel. 93000-31060

Travelling by Air

International Airport Wien-Schwechat (19 km south-east of the city centre), Tel. 7007-22233 (information available 24 hours). The fastest way from Landstrasse/Wien Mitte to the airport is the City Airport Train (CAT), which takes 16 minutes and costs Euro 9. Or you take the S-Bahn (Schnellbahn)/train S 7.

Airlines

Austrian Airlines: 1st District, Kärntner Ring 18; Tel. 05/1789, Fax 05/1766-4230; Flughafen (airport) Schwechat, Tel. 7007-6111, Fax 7007-69352

Air France: 1st District, Kärntner Strasse 49, Tel. 50222-2400 (reservation), Fax 5139426

Alitalia: 1st District, Kärntner Ring 2, Tel. 5051707-0; Flughafen (airport) Schwechat, Tel. 7007-32643

British Airways: 1st District, Kärntner Ring 10, Tel. 79567-567 and 5057696, Fax 5042084; Flughafen (airport) Schwechat, Tel. 7007-32646

KLM: 1st District, Kärntner Strasse 23, Tel. 51646, Fax 51646-34

Lufthansa: 6th District, Mariahilfer Strasse 123, Tel. 0810/10258080

Lauda Air: 1st District, Opernring 6, Tel. 7000-76730; Flughafen (airport) Schwechat, Tel. 7000-777, Fax 7000-5777

Swiss International Air Lines: 1st District, Marc-Aurel-Strasse 4, Tel. 0810/810840; Flughafen (airport) Schwechat, Tel. 7007-35501

Austrian Airtransport (domestic flights): 10th District, Fontanastrasse 1, Tel. 05/1789

City Traffic

As parking facilities in the Inner City are very limited, it is better to park your car outside the centre (parking lots, multistorey car parks, Park + Ride) and then use public transport! It is possible to drive straight to hotels in the city centre – you will be shown to the nearest parking facility.

In **Districts 1 to 9** and **20** there is **short-term pay parking**: 1st District (Old City): Mon-Fri 9 am-7 pm (except holidays), maximum parking 1½ hrs. Districts 2 to 9 and 20: Mon-Fri 9 am-8 pm (except holidays), maximum parking 2 hrs. Fill in the short-stay parking ticket and put it behind the windscreen. You can obtain these tickets ("Kurzparkscheine") in all banks, in many "Tabak-Trafik" (tobacconist's) and in the Vienna Public Transit Services advance booking offices ("Vorverkaufsstellen der Wiener Linien"). Disabled people may park in these zones for as long as they wish (the ID should be placed behind the windscreen!).

Multistorey car parks in the 1st District (selection)

Parkhaus City: Wollzeile 7, entrance at Stephansplatz, behind the Cathedral; Opern-Garage: Kärntner Strasse 51 (with direct access to the Opera

House); Garage am Hof; Garage Wipark: Freyung; Rathauspark-Garage: Dr.-Karl-Lueger-Ring; Votiv-park-Garage: Schottenring-subway, entrance Universitätsstrasse); Garage am Beethovenplatz: entrance corner of Kantgasse and Fichtegasse; Garage am Schwedenplatz: entrance Marc-Aurel-Strasse

Public Transport

You can get anywhere in Vienna quickly and easily by underground, S-Bahn, tram or bus – and it is not even expensive! Children under 6 years of age ride free of charge. It is best to buy tickets in advance. These can be purchased from the Vienna Public Transit Service (Wiener Verkehrsbetriebe) and in tobacco shops.

Ticket selection:

24-hour pass, 72-hour pass, 8-day multiple ticket, "Streifenkarte" (can be used by several people – one strip is used per person per day), weekly pass, multiple ticket (4 strips) and single tickets (in a block containing 5 tickets). Single tickets can also be purchased in the means of transport used (ticket machines for which you need coins). These are, however, considerably more expensive.

Operating hours: trams from about 5/5:30 am to 11 pm/midnight, U-Bahn from about 5 am to midnight, buses usually from 6:30 am. Night buses run between half past midnight and 4 am in the nights Fri to Sat, Sat to Sun and before holidays. **Night bus lines (Nightliner)** operate between the outer districts and Schwedenplatz in the centre (tickets only available from ticket machines on the bus).

Pay less with the Vienna Card. Vienna becomes even more attractive for you. Get on and off the U-Bahn, bus and streetcar as you like (for 72 hours). Enjoy reductions on admission to attractions and museums and many other advantages. The Vienna Card is obtainable from your Vienna hotel, at the tourist information points and wherever tickets for Vienna public transportation are sold.

Information Service of the Vienna Public Lines

www.wienerlinien.at
Direction, 3rd District, Erdbergstrasse 202, Tel. 7909-0 and 7909-105
1st District, Karlsplatz, pedestrian subway, Tel. 5873186; Mon-Fri 6:30 am-6:30 pm, Sat, Sun, holidays 8:30 am-4 pm
1st District, Stephansplatz, Tel. 5124227; Mon-Fri 6:30 am-6:30 pm, Sat, Sun holidays 8:30 am-4 pm
2nd District, Praterstern, Tel. 249302; Mon-Fri 7 am-6:30 pm
3rd District, Landstrasse, Tel. 7120548; Mon-Fri 7 am-6:30 pm
7th District, Volkstheater, Tel. 5234881; Mon-Fri 7 am-6:30 pm
12th District, Philadelphiabrücke, Tel. 8138401; Mon-Fri 8 am-6 pm
15th District, Westbahnhof, Tel. 8940261; Mon-Fri 6:30 am-6:30 pm, Sat, Sun holidays 8:30 am-4 pm
21st District, Floridsdorf, U-Bahnstation, Mon-Fri 6:30 am-6:30 pm

Interconnecting Transport System Eastern Region (Verkehrsverbund Ost-Region: VOR):

6th District, Maria Hilferstraße 77-79, Tel. 5266048
VOR-Info Hotline, Tel. 0810/222324 (local call)
Map of public transport network available at the information and advance-booking offices of the Vienna Public lines.

Taxis

There are over 100 taxi stands that can be reached by telephone throughout the city Radio Taxi headquarters: 23rd District, Pfarrgasse 54; Tel. 40100

Rapid transit system · Regional-, Schnell- und U-Bahnlinien · Lignes de communication rapide
Linee di comunicazione veloce · Systém rychlé dopravy · Gyorsforgalmú összeköttetések

VOR ⟵⟶

Schnell- und Regionalbahnlinie mit Station
Schnellbahnlinie mit Station
Regionalbahnlinie mit Station
U-Bahnlinie mit Station
Lokalbahn Wien-Baden mit Station

S 50 Linienbezeichnung Schnellbahn
R 50 Linienbezeichnung Regionalbahn
U1 U2 U3 U4 U6 Linienbezeichnung U-Bahn

⟵ siehe ÖBB-Fahrpläne

© Verkehrsverbund Ost-Region (VOR)
Gesellschaft m.b.H.
A-1060 Wien, Mariahilfer Straße 77-79
Auskünfte: 01/526 60 48-0
0810 22 23 24
Die Hotline, die Sie weiterbringt.
www.vor.at
wap.vor.at
Ihre Fahrplanauskunft online.

VOR TD-01/7, 10.2003, VOR SD-01/6, 10.2003
Graphik: Ennsfellner Consulting

Laa an der Thaya Stadt
R20
Laa an der Thaya
Kottingneusiedl
Staatz
Enzersdorf bei Staatz
Frättingsdorf
Hörersdorf
Siebenhirten Haltestelle
Mistelbach
Paasdorf
Ladendorf
Neubau-Kreuzstetten
Niederkreuzstetten
Hautzendorf
Schlenbach
Ulrichskirchen
Wolkersdorf
Obersdorf
R18
Seyring
Kapellerfeld
Gerasdorf

Gänserndorf Brünner Straße
R18
Gaweinstal
Kollnbrunn
Pürawarth
Pillichsdorf

Hohenruppersdorf
R18
Klein Harras
Bad Pirawarth
Groß Schweinbarth
Großengersdorf
Bockfließ
Auersthal
Raggendorf Markt
Raggendorf
Matzen
Prottes

Bernhardsthal
R15
Rabensburg
Hohenau
Drösing
Sierndorf an der March
Jedenspeigen
Dürnkrut
Stillfried
Angern
Tallesbrunn
Weikendorf-Dörfles

Floridsdorf
Siemensstraße
Neue Donau

Leopoldau
Süßenbrunn
Deutsch Wagram
Helmahof
Strasshof
Silberwald

Gänserndorf
Weikendorf
Stripfing
Oberweiden
Siebenbrunn/Leopoldsdorf
Untersiebenbrunn
Schönfeld-Lassee
Breitensee
Marchegg

R17
R80

Handelskai
Dresdner Straße
Jägerstraße
Spittelau
Friedensbrücke
Josefs-Bahnhof
R40
R42

Kagran
Alte Donau
Kaisermühlen-
Vienna Int. Centre
Donauinsel
Breitenleer Straße
Erzherzog-Karl-Straße
Hirschstetten
Handelsstraße
Raasdorf
Glinzendorf

S80
Stadlau

Straße
Roßauer Lände
Schottentor-
Universität
Schottenring
U2
Rathaus
Herrengasse
Nestroyplatz
Vorgartenstraße
Wien Nord/Praterstern
R15 R30
Schwedenplatz

Volkstheater
Stephansplatz
Stubentor
Museumsquartier
r Straße
Oper
U2
Stadtpark
Karlsplatz
Paulanergasse
Rennweg
Mayerhofgasse
Zipererstraße
Taubstummengasse
Kettenbrücken-
gasse
Johann-Strauß-Gasse
St. Marx
St. Marx
Geiselbergstraße
Simmering
Wien Mitte/Landstraße
Rochusgasse
Kardinal-Nagl-Platz
Schlachthausgasse
Erdberg
Gasometer
Erdberg
Enkplatz U3
Haidestraße

Lobau
Praterkai

Laurenzgasse
Kliebergasse
R10 R11
R13 R61
Keplerplatz
Reumannplatz
U1
Süd
S2 DIRECT
R2 S3 S7
R3 S60 R67
Kaiserebersdorf
Grillgasse
Klederinggasse

Zentralfriedhof
Kaiserebersdorf
Schwechat
Mannswörth
Flughafen Wien (VIE)
Fischamend
Maria Ellend an der Donau
Haslau
Regelsbrunn
Petronell-Carnuntum
Bad Deutsch Altenburg
Hainburg/Donau Frachtenbhf
Hainburg/Donau Personenbhf
Hainburg/Ungartor

Whitethal
S7

Blumental
Hennersdorf
Maria Lanzendorf
Lanzendorf-
Rannersdorf
Himberg
Gramatneusiedl
Götzendorf
Trautmannsdorf an der Leitha
Sarasdorf
Wilfleinsdorf
Bruck an der Leitha
Pandorf Ort-Neudorf
Gattendorf
Parndorf
Zurndorf

Parna
Pama
Nickelsdorf
Wiese R67
R65

Achau
Münchendorf
Ebreichsdorf
Wampersdorf
Pottendorf-
Landegg
Neusiedl an der Leitha
Mittlendorf

Neusiedl am See
S60 R63
Jois
Winden
Breitenbrunn
Purbach am Neusiedlersee
Donnerskirchen
Schützen Haltestelle
Schützen am Gebirge
Eisenstadt Schule
Eisenstadt
Wulkaprodersdorf Haltestelle
Wulkaprodersdorf
R63
Draßburg
Baumgarten
Sopron/Ungarn
Deutschkreutz
R13 R14

Bad Neusiedl am See
Weiden am See
Gols
Mönchhof Haltestelle
Mönchhof-Halbturn
Frauenkirchen
Sankt Andrä am Zicksee
Wallern im Burgenland
Pamhagen
R64

Nord
Mattersburg
Marz Rohrbach
Loipersbach-
Schattendorf

91

Nightlines

(Public transportation
from Sun night to Fri morning)

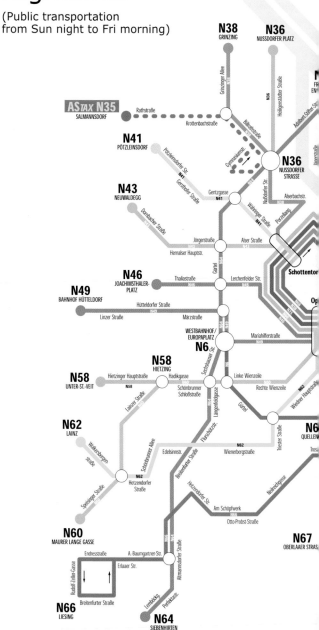

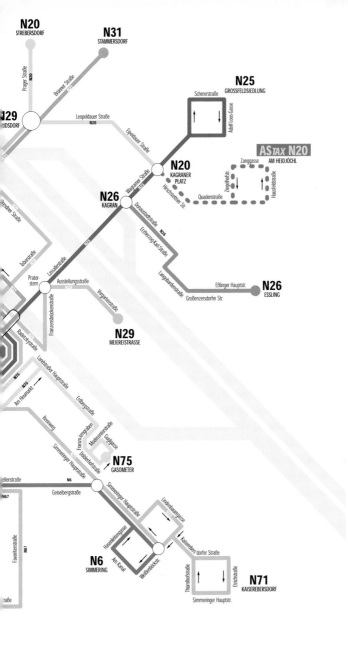

N20 STREBERSDORF

N31 STAMMERSDORF

N25 GROSSFELDSIEDLUNG

Prager Straße

Brünner Straße

N29 ...DSDORF

Leopoldauer Straße

Schererstraße

Adolf Loos-Gasse

ASTAX N20 AM HEIDJÖCHL

Zanggasse

Eipeldauer Straße

N20 KAGRANER PLATZ

Ziegelhofstr.

Hausfeldstraße

Wagramer Straße

Quadenstraße

N26 KAGRAN

Hirschstettner Str.

Donaustadtstraße

...reicher Straße

Erzherzog-Karl-Straße

Jabostraße

Langobardenstraße

Prater- stern

Lokalbahnstraße

Ausstellungsstraße

Eßlinger Hauptstr.

N26 ESSLING

Vegartenstraße

Großenzersdorfer Str.

Franzendruckerstraße

N29 MEIEREISTRASSE

Radetzkystraße

Landstraßer Hauptstraße

Erdbergstraße

Am Heumarkt

Rennweg

Franzosengraben

Modecenterstraße

Gürgasse

Simmeringer Hauptstraße

Dobleholzstraße

N75 GASOMETER

...ellenstraße

N6

Geiselbergstraße

Simmeringer Hauptstraße

N67

Lindenbauergasse

Hasenleitengasse

Kaiserebersdorfer Straße

Favoritenstraße

N6 SIMMERING

Am Kanal

Weißenböckstr.

Thürnhofstraße

Etrichstraße

N71 KAISEREBERSDORF

Simmeringer Hauptstr.

...traße

Großmarkt

Fried, breaded chicken, traditional Viennese cuisine

Food and Drink

Vienna offers numerous gastronomic opportunities. From restaurants of all price classes, where the selection extends from typical Viennese cuisine to foreign specialities, to old Viennese inns and "Beisl" (old original Viennese inns frequented by the man in the street, simple and cheap), coffeehouses, rich in tradition, and finally – you cannot come to Vienna without a visit here – the "heurige" (pub where new wine is served). There is one disadvantage: many restaurants are closed on Sunday. Visitors can obtain a good overview of culinary opportunities from a restaurant information brochure (Shopping, Wining & Dining) provided by the Vienna Tourist Office. A small selection is given here:

Restaurants

Altes Fassl, 5th District, Ziegelofen-gasse 37; Tel. 5444298; closed Mon
Altwiener Hof, 15th District, Herklotzgasse 6; Tel. 8926000 (luxury class, French cuisine); closed Sun
Bei Max, 1st District, Landhausgasse 2; Tel. 5337359
Drei Husaren, 1st District, Weih-burggasse 4; Tel. 5121092 (luxury class)
Figlmüller, 1st District, Wollzeile 5; Tel. 5126177
Hauswirth, 6h District, Otto-Bauer-Gasse 20; Tel. 5871261 (upper price range); closed Sun
Hopferl, 1st District, Naglergasse 13; Tel. 5332641; closed Sun
Korso, 1st District, Mahlerstrasse 2 (Hotel Bristol, luxury class); Tel. 51516-546

Ofenloch, 1st District, Kurrentgasse 8; Tel. 5338844
Oswald und Kalb, 1st District, Bäckerstrasse 14; Tel. 5121371; evenings only
Rimini, 5th District, Hauslabgasse 23; Tel. 5444356; closed Sun, Mon
Salm Bräu, 3rd District, Rennweg 8; Tel. 7995992
Steirereck, 3rd District, Rasumofskygasse 2 (luxury class); Tel. 7133168; closed Sat and Sun
Urbani Keller, 1st District, Am Hof 12; Tel. 5339102 (featuring zither music)

Coffehouses
Bräunerhof, 1st District, Stallburggasse 2; Tel. 5123893
Central, 1st District, Herrengasse 14 (Palais Ferstel); Tel. 5333763; closed Sun
Drechsler, 6th District, Linke Wienzeile 22; Tel. 5878580; closed Sun
Eiles, 8th District, Josefstädter Strasse 2; Tel. 4053410
Gloriette, 13rd District, Schlosspark Schönbrunn; Tel. 8791311

Hawelka, 1st District, Dorotheergasse 6; Tel. 5128230; closed Sun morning and Tue
Landtmann, 1st District, Dr.-Karl-Lueger-Ring 4; Tel. 5320621-0
Museum, 1st District, Friedrichstrasse 6; Tel. 5865202
Sacher, 1st District, Philharmonikerstrasse 4; Tel. 5121487
Sperl, 6th District, Gumpendorfer Strasse 11; Tel. 5864158; closed Sun morning
Tirolerhof, 1st District, Tegetthoffstrasse 8; Tel. 5127833
Wortner, 4th District, Wiedner Hauptstrasse 55; Tel. 9690491

Culinary tip: original recipes from Viennese cuisine are included in the booklets **Austrian Pastries and Desserts** *(No. 1717) and* **Austrian Specialties** *(No. 1718) and* **Viennese Specialties** *(No. 1716), KOMPASS "Kitchen Delights", published by KOMPASS-Karten GmbH.*

Heurige

There are many such "heurige" in the old wine-growing villages on the outskirts of Vienna such as Grinzing, Sievering, Neustift, Heiligenstadt, Nussdorf, Grossjedlersdorf, Mauer, Oberlaa, Ottakring or Stammersdorf and Strebersdorf. They all have the typical Viennese heurige atmosphere and serve wine from the most recent vintage (Heuriger); you can also help yourself to a small snack from the buffet.

Having a good time at the heurigen

Nightspots, Pubs

Aera, 1st District, Gonzagagasse 11; Tel. 5335314

Das Möbel, 7th District, Burggasse 10; Tel. 5249497

Daun-Kinsky, 1st District, Freyung 4; Tel. 5326271-21

Depot, 7th District, Breite Gasse 3; Tel. 5227613

Do & Co., 1st District, Stephansplatz 12/Haas-Haus, 7th floor; Tel. 5353969

Europa Hinterzimmer, 7th District, Zollergasse 8; Tel. 5238914

Halle, 7th District, Museumsplatz 1/ MuseumsQuartier (MQ); Tel. 5237001

Hansen, 1st District, Wipplingerstrasse 34; Tel. 5320542

Horvath, 5th District, Hamburger Strasse 2; Tel. 5857300

Krah Krah, 1st District, Rabensteig 8; Tel. 5338193

Livingstone, 1st District, Zelinkagasse 4; Tel. 5333393-12

Lux, 7th District, Schrankgasse 4/Spittelberggasse 3; Tel. 5269491

MAK Café (Austrian Museum of the Applied Arts), 1st District, Stubenring 5; Tel. 7140121

Palmenhaus im Burggarten, 1st District, Burggarten/Entrance Albertina, Tel. 5331033

Panigl, 8th District, Josefstädter Strasse 91; Tel. 4065218

Planter's Club, 1st District, Zelinkagasse 4; Tel. 5333393-15

rhiz bar modern, 8th District, Lerchenfelder Gürtel/Bögen 37/38; Tel. 4092505

Salzamt, 1st District, Ruprechtsplatz 1; Tel. 5335332; evennings only

Salz und Pfeffer, 6th District, Joanelligasse 8; Tel. 5866660; evenings only

Vorstadt, 16th District, Herbststrasse 37; Tel. 4931788

WUK, 9th District, Währinger Strasse 59; Tel. 40121-0

Bars, Discos, Cafés with Dancing

Blaue Bar, Hotel Sacher, 1st District, Philharmonikerstrasse 4; Tel. 51456-0

Broadway Piano-Bar, 1st District, Bauernmarkt 21; Tel. 5332849; closed Sun

Club U im Otto-Wagner-Cafe, 1st District, Karlsplatz/Künstlerhauspassage; Tel. 5059904

Eden-Bar, 1st District, Liliengasse 2; Tel. 5127450

Flex, 1st District, Donaukanal/Augartenbrücke; Tel. 5337525

Jenseits Tanzcafé, 6th District, Nelkengasse 3; Tel. 5871233

Kunsthalle Cafe, 4th District, Treitlstrasse 1-3; Tel. 5869864

Porgy & Bess, 1st District, Riemergasse 11; Tel. 5128811

Schikaneder Bar, 4th District, Margaretenstrasse 22-24; Tel. 5855888

Volksgarten, 1st District, Burgring 1; Tel. 5330518

Jazz, Live Music

Jazzland, 1st District, Franz-Josefs-Kai 29; Tel. 5332575, closed Sun and Mon

Papa's Tapas, 4th District, Schwarzenbergplatz 10; Tel. 5050311

Cabarets

Akzent, 4th District, Theresianumgasse 18; Tel. 50165-3306

Freie Bühne Wieden, 4th District, Wiedner Hauptstrasse 60b; Tel. 5862122

Kabarett Niedermair, 8th District, Lenaugasse 1a; Tel. 4084492

Kabarett Simpl, 1st District, Wollzeile 36; Tel. 5124742

Kulisse, 17th District, Rosensteingasse 39; Tel. 4853870

Metropol, 17th District, Hernalser Hauptstrasse 55; Tel. 4077740-7

Spektakel, 5th District, Hamburger Strasse 14; Tel. 5870653

Stadnikow, 1st District, Biberstrasse 2; Tel. 5125400

Vindobona, 20th District, Wallensteinplatz 6; Tel. 3324231 (Book tickets in advance)

Cinemas

Bellaria, 7th District, Museumstrasse 3, Tel. 5237591

Burgkino, 1st District, Opernring 19; Tel. 5878406

Gartenbau, 1st District, Parkring 12; Tel. 5122354

Metro, 1st District, Johannesgasse 4; Tel. 5121803

Österreichisches Filmmuseum (Austrian Museum of Films), 1st District, Augustinerstrasse 1; Tel. 5337056

Stadtkino, 3rd District, Schwarzenbergplatz 7; Tel. 7126276

Votiv, 9th District, Währinger Strasse 12; Tel. 3173571

Cinemas showing films in English

De France, 1st District, Schottenring 5, Eingang Hessgasse, Tel. 345236

Burg-Kino, 1st District, Opernring 19, Tel. 5878406

Top Kino Center, 6th District, Rahlgasse 1, Tel. 5875557

Concerts

Konzerthaus, 3rd District, Lothringer Strasse 20; Tel. 24200. Box office: Mon-Fri 9 am-6 pm, Sat 9 am-1 pm

Musikverein, 1st District, Bösendorfer Strasse 12; Tel. 5058681. Box office: Mon-Fri 9 am-6 pm, Sat 9-noon

Opera House and Theatres

www.cultureall.com (online ticket sales for all federal theaters)

The most important of Vienna's 50-odd theatres:

Akademietheater, 3rd District, Lisztstrasse 1; Tel. 51444-4140

Interior of the Vienna State Opera

Ateliertheater, 7th District, Burggasse 71; Tel. 5242245
Burgtheater (National Theatre), 1st District, Dr.-Karl-Lueger-Ring 2; Tel. 51444-4140
Kammerspiele, 1st District, Rotenturmstrasse 20; Tel. 42700
Raimundtheater, 6th District, Wallgasse 18; Tel. 59977-0
Ronacher, 1st District, Himmelpfortgasse 25; Tel. 51411
Schauspielhaus, 9th District, Porzellangasse 19; Tel. 3170101
Schönbrunner Schlosstheater, 13th District, Schloss Schönbrunn; Tel. 8173247
Staatsoper (State Opera), 1st District, Opernring 2; Tel. 51444-2250
Theater an der Wien, 6th District, Linke Wienzeile 6; Tel. 58830-0
Theater in der Josefstadt, 8th District, Josefstädter Strasse 26; Tel. 42700

Vienna's English Theatre,
8th District, Josefsgasse 12; Tel. 4021260

Volksoper (Comic Opera), 9th District, Währinger Strasse 78; Tel. 51444-3670
Volkstheater, 7th District, Neustiftgasse 1; Tel. 5233501
Wiener Kammeroper, 1st District, Fleischmarkt 24; Tel. 5120100

Ticket Sales: Tickets must be ordered in writing for the Staatsoper, Volksoper, Burg- and Akademietheater (3 weeks in advance): Austrian Federal Theatre Association (Österreichischer Bundestheaterverband, 1st District, Goethegasse 1, Tel. 51444-0. Payment with credit card (no earlier than 7 days before performance, Tel. 5131513). Box office (not earlier than 7 days before performance): 1st District, Hanuschgasse 3; Mon-Fri 8 am-6 pm, Sat 9 am-2 pm, Sun and holidays 9 am-noon. Written ticket orders for Theater in der Josefstadt and Kammerspiele: Theater in der Josefstadt, 8th District, Josefstädter Strasse 26. Box office: daily

9 am-6 pm. Tel. 42700-300.
Written ticket orders for Theater an der Wien und Raimundtheater (1 month in advance): Vienna Ticket Service, 1st District, Börsegasse 1, Tel. 53417-0, Fax 53417-26. Box office: 6th District, Linke Wienzeile 6; Tel. 58830-0; daily 10 am-1 pm and 2-6 pm.

Information as to **programmes** and available tickets (recorded message): Tel. 1518. Regular season: 1st Sept to 30th June

"Son-et-Lumière"
This Sound-Light-Show about the history of the palace takes place in the park of the Upper Belvedere in the summer (9:30 pm)
3rd District, Oberes Belvedere, Prinz-Eugen-Strasse 27;
Tel. 79557-134

Municipal Libraries
Main library: 8th District, Skoda-gasse 20; Tel. 4000-13 and 4000-8450. For further libraries see telephone directory

Casino
1st District, Kärntner Strasse 41; Tel. 5124836

Events throughout the year

For calendar of events see www.wien.info

January
New Year: the Vienna Philharmonic Orchestra's New Year's Concert in the Musikvereins concert hall; Beethoven's 9th Symphony with the Vienna Symphony Orchestra.
The Hunters' Ball (Jägerball), the Vienna Philharmonic Orchestras Ball, the Vienna Doctors' Ball (Ärzteball), the Flower Ball (Blumenball). Resonanzen (Festival of Ancient Music).

The Opera Ball

February
Masked Ball at Vienna's imperial court, Artists' Ball (Künstlerball), Bonbonball, Magicians' Ball, Lawyers' Ball (Juristenball) etc. The culmination is the Opera Ball on the Thursday before "Faschingssonntag" (the last Sunday in carneval); carneval procession; Vienna Dance Weeks (to March); Vienna Dream on Ice (public ice-skating to music at Rathausplatz, end of January to early March).

March
Haydn Days; Viennale Film Festival, Hernalser Kalvarienberg Market, Vienna Spring Fair; performances by the Spanish Riding School (March to June).

April
Sacred Music Days; waltz and operetta concerts (April to October); OsterKlang

Wien (Easter Music Festival); Frühlingsfestival (Spring Festival, Konzerthaus or Musikverein, April to early May).

May
Vienna City Marathon; City Festival; Vienna Festival Weeks (Konzerthaus, MuseumsQuartier Vienna, Theater an der Wien and many other venues, May/June); Spring Festival at Prater.

Vienna City Marathon

June
Floral Parade at Prater; Brass Band Music Festival; Concordia Ball; University Ball; Austrian Horse Riding Derby in Freudenau; Fashion Show by the City of Vienna's School of Fashion in Palace Hetzendorf; "Klangbogen" Vienna Music Summer (June to mid-August); Danube Island Festival; VINOVA International Wine Fair.

July
Jazz Festival (State Opera, one open air location, several jazz clubs; end of June to Mid-July); Spectaculum; International Youth & Music Festival (Austria Center, beginning of July); Music Film Festival on Rathausplatz (July, August); Summer Theatre (July, August); The City of Vienna Prize in

Freudenau (horse race); ImPulsDance Festival (MuseumsQuartier Vienna, Volkstheater and other venues); Klang-Bogen Festival (Theater an der Wien, Musikverein and various other venues, July to August).

August
Prater Fair

September
Vienna Autumn Trade Fair; Spanish Riding School (performances to December); Prater People's Festival; Poschacher Commemorative Race (Trotting Race Club Krieau); Mass with the Vienna Boys' Choir (Sept to July).

October
Image, Dance in Künstlerhaus (1st-26th); Keep Fit Walks on Austria's National Holiday (26th); Vienna Modern, Festival for 20th Century Music in Konzerthaus (to the beginning of December); Earl Kálmán Hunyady-Memorial Race (Trotting Race Club Krieau); Austrian Book Week in the City Hall; Viennale Film Festival; Jeunesse Festival.

November
Schubertiade; Antiques Fair; Display of Antiques in the Kursalon; Horse Festival, International Riding and Jumping Competition in the City Arena (Stadthalle); Crib Display in St. Peter's Church and Christmas Exhibition at the City Hall (mid-Nov to 24th Dec); Champagne Ball in the Hofburg.

December
"Christkindlmarkt" (Christmas Market) on Rathausplatz (in front of the City Hall); Old Vienna Christkindlmarkt at Freyung; Christmas Market on Spittelberg; Mozart Festival in the Concert Hall; International Indoor Football Tournament in the City Hall; 31st Dec: Kaiserball (Emperor's Ball) in the Hofburg, New Year's Concert with the Vienna Philharmonic Orchestra in the Musikverein, New Year's performance of the "Fledermaus" ("The Bat") at the State Opera. New Year's Party on Stephansplatz.

SPORT

Information about all popular types of sport, sports grounds, equipment rental can be acquired at:
Vienna Xtra Jugendinfo, 1st District, Babenbergerstrasse 1; Tel. 1799 (Mon-Fri noon-7 pm, Sat 10 am-7 pm). Internet surfing for young people.

Equestrian Sport
Race tracks
Freudenau (Vienna Horse Racing Club), 2nd District, Freudenau 65, Rennbahnstrasse; Tel. 7289535
Krieau (Vienna Horse Racing Club), 2nd District, Nordportalstrasse 247; Tel. 7280046-0

Riding
Information: Landesfachverband für Reiten und Fahren in Wien,
1st District, Hofburg, Batthyány-stiege; Tel. 5337046

Riding Clubs
Reitclub Donau und Reitclub Donauhof, 2nd District, Hafenzufahrt-strasse 63
Reitclub Donaustadt, 22nd District, Campingplatzweg/Parz. 247

Reit- und Fahrclub Tarpan, 22nd District, Stadlbreitengasse
Reitverein Freudenau, 2nd District, Freudenau 555
Reitverein Prater, 2nd District, Dammhaufen 62
Reitzentrum Wien-Nord, 22nd District, Zwerchäckerweg 28
Union Reit- und Fahrverein St. Stephan, 22nd District, Weingartenallee 18
Wiener Reitinstitut, 3rd District, Barmherzigengasse 17

Fitnesscenter
Fitness im MBC Sport- und Erho-lungspark Am Wiener Berg, 10th District, Gutheil-Schoder-Gasse 9; Tel. 66123
Fitness in der Sportarena, 22nd District, Bernouillistrasse 7; Tel. 2023400
Fitness in der Sportcenter Top Ten, 2st District, Jedlersdorfer Strasse 94; Tel. 2924040
Fitness-Studio Olympia, Schwechat, Himberger Strasse 11; Tel. 7072690
Fitness-Center Donaupark, 22nd District, Arbeiterstrandbadstrasse 122; Tel. 2633450
City Fitness, 7th District, Kaiser-strasse 43; Tel. 5262000

Golf
Golf Club Schönfeld, 2nd District, Obere Donaustrasse 97/Stiege 1; Tel. 2161320
Golfclub Am Wienerberg, 1st District, Gutheil-Schoder-Gasse 6-9; Tel. 66123
Golf Club Wien, 2nd District, Freudenau 65a; Tel. 7289564
Golf Club 2000 Sportanlagen, 2nd District; Krieau, Tel. 7260560
Information: Österr. Golfverband, Haus des Sports, 4th District,

Prinz-Eugen-Strasse 12;
Tel. 5053245

Ice-skating
Brigittenauer Sporthalle,
20th District, Brigittenauer
Lände 236; Tel. 3305295
Eisring Süd (Ice-rink south),
10th District, Windtenstrasse 2;
Tel. 6044443
Kunsteisbahn Donauparkhalle,
22nd District, Wagramer Strasse 1
Kunsteisbahn Engelmann,
17th District, Syringgasse 6-8;
Tel. 4051425
Wiener Eislaufverein, 3rd District,
Lothringerstrasse 22; Tel. 7136353
Wiener Stadthalle (Vienna City Hall),
Halle C, 15th District, Vogelweidplatz
14; Tel. 98100-208

Rowing
Information: Wiener Ruderverband,
22nd District, Florian-Berndl-Gasse 3;
Tel. 2034879; Mon-Fri 3-5 pm

Sailing, Surfing
Vienna Yacht Club, 21st District,
An der Oberen Alten Donau 92
Sailing Centre New Danube, Danube
Island, Tel. 2786385
Information: Landes-Segelverband für
Wien, A-1033 Wien, Box 160

Soccer
Ernst-Happel-Stadion, Prater, 2nd
District, Meiereistrasse 7;
Tel. 7280854
Information: Österr. Fußballbund
(ÖFB), 2nd District, Meiereistrasse 7;
Tel. 72718-0

Swimming
For pool opening hours call the Municipal Pool Administration, 10th District, Reumannplatz 23,
Tel. 60112

In Vienna there are several **indoor
swimming pools** (some of which also have open-air pools) that are open
all year round:
Amalienbad (renovated Jugend-

stilpool), 10th District, Reumannplatz
Dianabad, 2nd District,
Lilienbrunnergasse
Hallenbad Floridsdorf, 21st District,
Franklinstrasse 22
Hallenbad/Freibad (indoor and out-
door pools) Döbling, 19th District,
Geweygasse 6
Hallenbad/Freibad Donaustadt,
22nd District, Portnergasse 38
Hallenbad/Freibad Grossfeldsiedlung,
21st District, Oswald-Redlich-Str. 44
Hallenbad/Freibad Hietzing,
13th District, Atzgersdorfer Strasse 14
Hallenbad/Freibad Ottakring,
16th District, Johann-Staud-Strasse 11
Hallenbad/Freibad Simmering,
11th District, Florian-Hedorfer-
Strasse 5 Jörgerbad, 17th District,
Jörgerstrasse 42-44
Schwimmbad Pratersauna,
2nd District, Waldsteingarten-
strasse 135
Sieveringer Bad, 19th District,
Sieveringer Strasse 267
Theresienbad, 12th District,
Hufelandgasse 3
Thermalbad/Freiluftbad Oberlaa,
10th District, Kurbadstrasse 14

There are also **summer swimming
pools** and **swimming facilities on
rivers** (Strandbäder). These are
mostly open from the beginning of
May to the middle of September:
Bundesbad Schönbrunn, 13th Dis-
trict, Schönbrunner Schlosspark
Bundessportbad Alte Donau, 22nd
District, Arbeiterstrandbadstrasse 93
Höpflerbad, 23rd District, Atzgers-
dorf, Endresstrasse 24-26
Kongressbad, 16th District, Julius-
Meinl-Gasse 7a
Krapfenwaldlbad, 19th District,
Krapfenwaldgasse 65-73
Laaer-Berg-Bad, 10th District,
Ludwig-von-Höhnel-Gasse 2
Liesinger Bad, 23rd District, Perch-
toldsdorfer Strasse 14-16